KARATE CLEVER

Searching for a New Way

Scott Langley

MASON PRESS

First published in 2016 by
Mason Press
Rear of Cullenswood Park
Ranelagh
Dublin 6]

CreateSpace paperback ISBN: 978 1 911013 549
eBook – mobi format ISBN: 978 1 911013 556
eBook – ePub format ISBN: 978 1 911013 563

Cover design by Gareth Jones, www.gazjonesdesign.com
Typesetting and layout by Dinky Typesetting and Design

KARATE CLEVER

For my dad

Bun Bu Ryo Do

In Japan *Bun Bu Ryo Do* is a famous saying. *Bun* means academic study. *Bu* means martial study. *Ryo* means together, and *Do* means the way. *Bun Bu Ryo Do* means only by training both the body and mind can you find the true way. This is my story of karate clever.

ONE

I approached the immigration officer with my back to Japan, ready to exit the country for the very last time.

'*Gaijin*[1] card, please.'

I handed over the ID card that foreigners were obliged to carry at all times.

'Thank you,' she said with finality, popping it into a drawer.

'But …' I held out my hand in the hope that she had made a mistake, but all I got in the way of an answer was a disapproving shake of the head. I walked through to the international area, newly stripped of my legal *gaijin* status. The date was 4 July 2002, exactly five years to the day that I first set foot in Japan.

If anyone was in need of a holiday, it was me. The Instructors' Course had physically and mentally scarred me, all for this vague, ethereal dream of one day being a professional instructor in Ireland. However, I had made it to the finishing line, becoming only the fifth foreigner to graduate in its sixty-year history. When Yumoto Sensei gave me the date of my graduation I started to plan. There was no way I was heading straight home. I deserved a little R & R. However, the reason I had given to Yumoto Sensei for having to leave Japan – financial pressures at home – was true. I had no money. Taking a holiday was somewhat problematic, so out

---

1. *Gaijin* – Foreigner, literally 'outside person'.

came my 'emergency' Barclaycard. I booked a month-long pass for Amtrak and a return ticket to Los Angeles; strangely, they wouldn't sell me a single ticket. At least *someone* in Japan didn't want me to leave.

I arrived before I left on the Fourth of July, passing the International Date Line, and gained twenty-four hours, which to this day no one has ever requested back. I cleared security, at that time quite a pleasant experience, jumped into a taxi and headed to Santa Monica where I checked into the local youth hostel. It wasn't the Ritz, but I could see the Hilton from the dormitory window, so that was close enough. I said hello to the others in the dorm, one of whom was Japanese. I spoke to him, but he pretended he couldn't understand me, even though my Japanese had been perfect twelve hours ago when I left Japan.

After sleeping off the jet lag, I spent the next few days wandering around Santa Monica, Hollywood and various other parts of the massive L.A. conurbation. It was a shock to the system, and everything Japan wasn't. Everyone was white. I hadn't seen so many *gaijin* in years. However, as I strolled into a nearby food mall on my first full day there, I quickly realized how segregated the USA is – facing me over the counter of every food outlet were black and Hispanic faces: whites were buying, blacks were selling. It was as stark as that. In a day I had gone from being the *gaijin* to being the majority, and strangely I started to feel very lonely. I rang home and remember my mum saying, 'Just enjoy yourself – relax.' My parents were bankrolling my jaunt, paying off my credit card as I went along, and I am sure after everything they had seen me go through, they couldn't fathom my current state of disquiet.

I roamed from one alien situation to another, and at one

point found myself on a bus tour of the 'Hollywood Homes of the Rich and Famous'. It was fun in a voyeuristic type of way. At one point we passed Nicholas Cage's house and the large wooden doors were open – people got whiplash trying to catch a glimpse of the car, although it has to be said that it was very shiny.

There were moments of enjoyment but the loneliness persisted. I didn't belong here and looked forward to getting out of L.A. and heading to Austin, Texas to see an old university friend, where I hoped the change of scenery and a familiar face would improve my state of mind. Maybe Japan has sunk into my core; maybe I was no longer 'Western'; maybe I shouldn't have left. *Maybe I shouldn't have left?* I had just spent the last two years literally counting down the days until I could leave. My emotions were in turmoil. In Japan, OCD and survival had dictated my existence and now, free from the constraints of my karate life, I struggled to be.

I sat on the floor of downtown L.A.'s palatial Union Station, the last of the great rail terminals, and made myself comfortable on the marble floor, typing away on an ancient laptop that Samantha had given me as a going-away present. In between organizing my Sayonara Party and taking me to a *Kyudo*[2] Dojo, she had convinced me that I should write a book and insisted I start it on my month-long trip across America. I wasn't hopeful, but I had promised her and had already typed a chapter outline. I was beginning to find it cathartic to write down what I had been through, and it was a way of escaping the waves of loneliness constantly taking me by surprise.

As I balanced my ancient Macintosh on my lap, a large woman with a thick African-American accent kicked my shoe. 'Hey buddy, what're you doing?' Squinting through the light,

2. *Kyudo* – Japanese archery

I made out she was a cop just in time to temper my response.

'Writing a book,' I replied, as if that were commonplace in L.A. And apparently it was. With a 'Sure, do it!' she turned on her heel and never bothered me again.

Half an hour later the same lady held back the crowd as a small Amtrak employee fended off questions. Apparently there had been massive flooding across western Texas. We could make it as far as El Paso, but ironically couldn't pass there. It would be onwards by coach. Everyone seemed very exercised about the whole affair, but I laboured under the false sense of security that five years of living in Japan had afforded me. What's the worst that could happen? A train, then a coach, seemed perfectly adequate.

I should have taken the hint when the official, who reminded me of Droopy the cartoon dog saying 'ticket please', meekly offered refunds, which most of the waiting crowd immediately accepted. However, as I was using my one-month Amtrak pass, I had nothing to be refunded and nowhere to stay in L.A. I was moving out.

Sixteen hours later I found myself in El Paso, expecting to jump on a coach to take me the remainder of the twenty-four-hour jaunt. We disembarked to discover an empty car park, so took down our luggage, waiting expectantly. In Japan, when something went wrong, apart from the compulsory *seppuku* [3]of a middle-ranking official, we always had ushers in white gloves determined to make our inconvenience as small as possible. In El Paso we had the sun and concrete to make our inconvenience as great as possible. Some passengers became cantankerous rather quickly, fluffing their feathers in a bid to make things happen, with the inevitable can-do American attitude. Others had the opposite reaction,

3. *Seppuku* – Ritual suicide

saying how preposterous these fools were, accepting their fate and carefully demonstrating how at peace they were at being stranded: these were more irritating than the 'peacocks', who, at least, were genuine. Most, thankfully, were sincerely at peace with their predicament and sat in resigned contemplation as we waited for our promised chariots.

El Paso, meaning 'the pass', is situated on the Rio Grande, but my childhood images of the famous river, scattered with cowboys herding cattle, were inevitably dashed. The Amtrak station stood within spitting distance of the Mexican border and as the hours passed I watched the life that existed on the other side of the fence. Mexico was poor and on average the difference between people on my side of the heavily fortified barrier and people on the other side was about $60,000 per person per year.

Eight hours later I heard the cheers before I saw the Greyhound buses – apparently Amtrak had called for the buses when we had arrived at El Paso, rather than sixteen hours earlier when we had left L.A. Maybe they were in two minds as to whether we would make it across the floods safely. Either way, it was no wonder they were on the verge of bankruptcy. I just hoped that they wouldn't go under until I had made it to the east coast.

As I boarded the coach, I found my seat next to a huge black guy. I had read an article a few days earlier in L.A. about Ebonics, the dialect of African-Americans, and had been fascinated by its official use in some of the inner-city school districts – I was about to get a crash course on the subject. Stanley, an extremely muscular gentleman, spoke with a rhythm that I wished I could understand, but alas, only every fourth or fifth word was accessible. Every time I spoke, I seemed to have fallen from a 1940s British war movie – 'I say, my good chap, that is sterling work' – as he showed me an exquisite portrait he had just finished of his fiancée. Stanley was an artist of some talent and thankfully we started to communicate, him through his sketches and me in P.G. Wodehouse clichés. 'The fascination of shooting as a sport depends almost wholly on whether you are at the right or wrong end of the gun,' I quoted as the bus driver called us to silence.

'Now,' he said with the authority bestowed on him by a cap and Greyhound badge, 'you've all seen the news.' My fellow travellers nodded knowingly. 'So I don't want any nonsense that happened a few days ago in Florida.' Everyone shook their heads in agreement. 'So no guns.' Stanley patted his left armpit, as if checking for something, and I regretted how our conversation had veered onto hunting. 'The toilets are at the back,' the driver continued, 'but no shooting up. And if you want to come and talk to me, you say, "Hey driver, I'm coming on up." And I'll say "Come on up!" But if anyone sneaks up on me, I'll slam on the brakes and you'll go straight through the windscreen.' Everyone again nodded, acknowledging the perfectly reasonable intention of our driver to kill anyone who 'sneaked'. He seemed to have more to say, but as he was planning on splattering our brains, a small Indian fellow got on the bus. Left arm raised high, he looked as if he had an important question. The driver greeted him with an officious 'Yes?'

'I have my train ticket,' he replied, wafting it with his other hand. He was pointed to a vacant seat and after he stowed his bag single-handedly, he sat, still with his arm raised. The driver looked again, waiting for the question to be asked, but none came. So, rather perplexed, he told us we were leaving and off we set for our eight-hour, non-stop trip to Austin.

The trip was uneventful, like any bus trip anywhere in the world. Stanley spiced it up with the occasional game of Guess What I'm Saying, and I was distracted frequently by checking if the Indian guy still had his hand up, which he did – for the entire eight hours. When we arrived in Austin he was the first off, bag in right hand. I watched him walk down the street as consecutive taxi drivers slowed down, thinking they were being hailed. He walked on oblivious. It was only years later that I found out there are some sadhus (Hindu holy men) who dedicate large parts of their life to keeping one of their arms aloft. One in particular, Amar Bharati, kept his arm raised for over forty years!

Paul, my old university karate buddy, was waiting patiently at the bus terminus. He had turned up eight hours earlier to find no train, had done a little detective work and managed to find me – oh, how we coped in the days before ubiquitous mobile phone cover and Facebook updates! 'How the hell are you?' he greeted me and gave me a massive whack on my arm – his girlfriend winced, muttered something unladylike, and gave him a withering look. 'He's fine,' he explained, 'he's just done the Instructors' Course'.

Despite the bruise on my upper arm, it was great to see Paul and the sense of loneliness dissipated very quickly. He had taken a few days off work and we cycled, walked, ate and drank our way around the beautiful city. It was modern, liberal and educated. At one point we walked around the state capitol building, which, when it was built 150 years ago, had been billed as the seventh-largest building in the world. However, within the Italian Renaissance-style structure I found George W. Bush's portrait hanging proudly on the wall, and it was only then that I realized how much of a conservative stronghold I found myself in. Austin seemed to be a cultural oasis amongst the deeply Republican state. As I relaxed, further recovered from jet lag and found my *gaijin* legs again, I realized that I had the strangest feeling being in America. I didn't belong. They spoke the same language as me. They ate the same food, watched the same films, TV programmes and listened to the same music, but these weren't my streets, these weren't my people. I thought my trip across America would be the reawakening of my Western self. I was starting to wonder if that side of me had been lost forever.

'What do you want to do tonight?' Paul was asking with a twinkle in his eye. 'Do you want to have some fun?' Fun was what I was here for. He mentioned The Landing Strip, Austin's premier gentlemen's club, and although I would have preferred chatting up women for real, I conceded to my host's recommendation. We went back to his apartment, a three-bedroom condo in a gated community. With a full-time reception, which boasted hot coffee and donuts freely available 24/7, the complex had a purpose-built gym, several swimming pools and security staff, all part of the service. Paul had a good job, but surely it wasn't that good. I could feel the wealth and although I had recently left the second-biggest economy in the world to arrive in the biggest, for me there was a stark difference between Japan and the USA. Unlike L.A., the staff were exclusively Hispanic, the residents middle-class whites and blacks. At a mere glance this distinction was unnoticeable; however, I felt it before I saw it. Something wasn't right.

Since that trip I have spent a lot of time in America and love the people and the place, but that separation of society is always there. In Japan the racism was obvious and blatant and I learnt to deal with it. In Japan you start out foreign, alien even, and slowly ingratiate yourself, becoming part of the group. In America you start off with everyone being your friend and then slowly realize the country is made up of closely knit groups that are impossible to penetrate.

I soon forgot about this conundrum as we entered a club full of beautiful women. After five years in Japan, experiencing the beauty of the Japanese form, this was something else. After one quick beer Paul turned to me and said, 'That beer went down well, I'm getting a real buzz now.'

'From the beer?' I asked. He nodded. How odd, I thought, as we launched into a conversation about how alcohol in the US is considered like any other drug. Of course it is, but to describe being drunk as getting a 'buzz' from the alcohol was strange. There was definitely a different attitude here. In America, maybe as a throwback to prohibition, there was no complete social acceptance of drink and this mindset influences and dictates everything from lawmakers legislating the highest drinking age in the world down to the way my university friend was feeling the buzz.

The conversation was interrupted by Rose, a stunning blonde, whose exquisite body was matched only by the beauty of her face. She sat down next to me and started to chat. She explained how she was a student doing this to pay her way through medical school – a cliché I would have dismissed as a lie if she hadn't been so wonderfully articulate and deeply interesting. After a while she must have remembered her job and asked if I wanted a dance. I declined for now, but said I would later. She left, giving me her stage name.

I said to Paul. 'I thought her name was Rose?'

'It is … she was really into you, that's why she gave you her real name. You should ask her out!' I hadn't seen that, I just thought she was being 'professionally' nice to me, so I frantically thought about how I could postpone my plan to move on to New Orleans in the morning and have a date with Rose.

I failed to formulate any strategy and then became distracted when Sally, Paul's girlfriend, arrived. 'We've been rumbled,' I muttered to Paul as we stood up. He looked at me, puzzled, and turned to hug and kiss Sally. Apparently the whole situation was perfectly normal. She sat with us and we enjoyed a pleasant evening of chat whilst being served by topless angels, the conversation occasionally punctuated with Sally watching Paul getting a lap dance and then Paul watching Sally getting a lap dance. I was so naive!

The next day I arrived in New Orleans, checked into the youth hostel and bumped into Johann, a Swedish guy. He was about my age and, like me, was travelling from the west coast to the east. We quickly agreed to explore New Orleans together and headed down to Bourbon Street: party central. Wild does not describe the scene that awaited us and I started to think that maybe prohibition never made it this far south. Mardi Gras was six months ago and we had timed it perfectly as this year's party was just drawing to a close whilst next year's party was starting. Everyone wore beaded necklaces of various colours and carried large soft-drink cups, although their general appearance hinted at something stronger than Mountain Dew.

We dived into the nearest bar and were immediately offered Hurricane cocktails. We ordered two and realized we were now the proud owners of a couple of the ubiquitous plastic cups. We were also given a necklace each and I started to wonder if the layers of beads around the necks of the people we'd seen was some sort of marker of alcohol consumed. We lashed into the Hurricanes and the explanation was given that the drink was invented when a storm hit the city: people were trapped in a certain bar and they ran out of the normal tipple, so had to get inventive, creating the cocktail that is now famous in the area. I have also heard that it was the invention of a speakeasy owner, Pat O'Brien, who wanted to get rid of cheap rum, and so invented the drink and served it in a 'hurricane' glass to unsuspecting sailors. I prefer the first explanation.

Whoever invented it did a terrific job. After three cocktails we moved on, drawn like moths to a bar flickering with neon. We walked in a beer-goggle paradise of beautiful southern belles chatting and dancing the night away. Before long my impressions of P.G. Wodehouse and Johann's impersonation of the Swedish chef from the Muppets afforded us many introductions. The night became rapidly foggy, but not in a meteorological sense. I lost Johann and found myself in the company of Heather, a cheerleader from California. Blonde, beautiful and British-mad, even I couldn't fuck this one up.

I staggered home in the early hours, wondering if this was a sensible idea: tiptoeing through a city that is one of the top ten most dangerous places to live in the US. But hey, I'm indestructible. I've just done the Instructors' Course, and with the amount of beads around my neck I looked like a Masai warrior.

From New Orleans I made my way up to Philadelphia. Mark, my French-Moroccan junior in Japan, had introduced me to the JKS affiliate there. During his eclectic childhood, Mark had lived in Philadelphia and started training at the dojo. Ron Sensei, a tall, athletic gentleman in his early fifties who could easily pass for late thirties, spoke with charismatic charm and a patter that I was coming to understand was one of the many endearing qualities of the black community in America. I had met him the year before at the international championships in Tokyo. We had stayed in touch and when I mentioned I would be travelling coast to coast, he insisted I made a visit.

I taught a crowded dojo, mostly black belts eager to see what I could do. I kept the lesson simple, as people seemed to move awkwardly and in a laboured fashion. Without doubt the participants were full of energy and enthusiasm, but they lacked fluidity and often seemed to be fighting against themselves to produce powerless shapes. In the coming years I would understand what was lacking in their karate, or more precisely, what Japan had given me in mine. For now, however, I kept it simple, trying not to patronize, but at the same time trying to teach them something of value. Ron Sensei was delighted. At the end of the class he came up, gave me a bear hug and announced to the group that the JKS was in good hands when producing instructors of my quality. They were happy so I was happy. All I had to do was replicate that reaction for the next forty years and all would be good.

'So Scott, what do you fancy doing now?' It was a Saturday night, we had trained hard and Ron Sensei was in charge. We were sitting in a Chinese restaurant, surrounded by the senior grades of the dojo, all of them young, energetic and in search of a good party. I had visions of a local bar with beautiful soulful goddesses gyrating in rhythm to the house band. My vision was quite specific, but as long as it involved a few beers and some fun with my new friends, I would be happy.

'Ron Sensei – whatever you want,' I replied expectantly.

'Okay.' He looked thoughtful. 'The cinema … I have been dying to see *Men in Black II*.'

I managed a half-hearted 'cool' and followed my leader as all the other seniors crossed the road, heading to a bar that seemed to be vibrating with the pulse of the party inside.

I realized that sometimes, as a karate instructor, I had to remember I was a paid employee, and the boss was the one paying my wage.

Although New York, my final destination, was a short train ride from Philly, I skipped the city and headed for Boston to meet Hiro, my old student and friend from Tokyo, who was now studying orthodontics at Harvard. A friendly face in a sea of strangers, I was relieved to see that his English was now high-level conversational. The eighteen months of twice-weekly lessons had been money well spent. He took me out for an expensive meal, although we ended up only eating starters as the portion sizes were so big, and we spent the next few evenings catching up. During the days I wandered around the old city: it reminded me of home; it had a European feel to it and I started to think of my return to England. I checked my Hotmail account and found a message waiting for me from Victoria. Tor – not a nickname but a strange Bristolian contraction of her name, VicTORia – had been the secretary of our university karate club and had then become Ladies' Captain of the British Team under Ishii Sensei. We had always been close, very close, but due to various issues with timing, we'd never got together. She was just letting me know she was looking forward to seeing me when I got home. 'Oh, I've also just split up from my boyfriend,' she added at the end. Timing was everything.

My time in the USA – and my parents' patience at my constant requests for more money – was drawing to a close. I headed to New York for the final week of my holiday. I had booked a single flight at a random travel agency, dumped my bags into the last youth hostel of my trip and took a stroll along Park Avenue. Manhattan only covers 33 square miles, but with nearly 70,000 people living on every square mile, it is vertically vast. I was used to Tokyo, but due to earthquakes there are no skyscrapers, and the city sprawls out as far as the eye could see. Manhattan was different. I called Richard Amos, my sempai[4] from Japan, who had now moved to New York.

'Where are you staying?' he asked. I answered, trying to sound cool by mentioning the Lower East Side. 'Nonsense, you can stay at the dojo.' Excellent, I thought. That was one less phone call I had to make home for more money.

During my time on the Instructors' Course, Richard Sempai had become *persona non grata* and my contact with him had been limited. In 1999, when our group lost the court case and was forced to change our name to JKS, several senior members of the group had split to form their own international groups: one became three and Richard Sempai had maintained strong links with all instructors. Torn, conflicted and proud to have always been JKA, he had decided to stay neutral: this hadn't gone down well with Yumoto Sensei, who never saw eye to eye with Richard Sempai. Yumoto Sensei gave him an ultimatum, which involved writing a letter of apology for his indecisiveness. This wasn't positively received and Richard Sempai walked away from what had been his karate home for over twenty-five years. The subject often came up whilst I was on the course in Japan. Richard was vilified as a *gaijin* without honour or loyalty. Although I never offered my opinion, I always wondered exactly who showed the most honour and loyalty in the whole situation.

Since leaving Japan, Richard had lost none of his sophistication and composure. I once described him as the James Bond of the karate world, and now he was the quintessential Englishman in New York – albeit not gay and

4. *Sempai* – One's senior

with the ability to kill you with one blow. He had a triplex apartment on the Upper East Side. The triplex style was the most expensive type of real estate in New York and the Upper East Side was the most expensive part of Manhattan: he seemed to be doing very well. The first floor was his living quarters, the second was his dojo and the third was his office and my bedroom for the few days I had left. We trained, wandered around Manhattan, ate and drank at exquisite bars

Enjoying a beer in Manhattan with Richard Amos (right) and his student (left), July 2002.

and restaurants and I was briefly afforded a glimpse of the life that I could build for myself in Dublin – maybe without the same sense of grandeur, extravagance, stylishness, weather and X factor that New York bestows upon you.

Richard Sempai had just become the Chief Instructor of the World Traditional Karate Organization. The WTKO was his answer to walking away from the JKS. He needed a group and a brand and this was it. The group was founded and chaired by John Mullin, a New York-based karate instructor of some renown. We met, trained and had lunch together. John had a great level and as a respected 7th dan[5], brought depth to the group. Back in Richard Sempai's dojo, John produced a sample of the new design for the WTKO logo.

'What do you think?' Richard Sempai asked. Of course, I wasn't going to be anything other than positive.

'It looks great,' I replied, genuinely impressed. Richard Sempai had been a huge influence in my life since I had first met him at seventeen. He had supported my acceptance onto the course and I wished him and John well with their new endeavour.

'Here, take this.' He handed me the sample of the WTKO badge. I took it with pride and thanked him – he was reaffirming our connection and all these years later I still have it.

The next day, after a crazy night out in TriBeCa, I boarded a plane and headed home for the first time in far too long. I faced great uncertainty. I had no money and still felt the West was alien. However, what I did have was a good karate level, my instructor's status and lots of energy. America may have failed to awaken my occidental side, but it had revitalized me and I landed in London proud and ready to build the JKS.

5. *Dan* – Level or diploma. Most think when you reach black belt, you are an expert. In fact it is the first of eight levels.

TWO

I arrived home with no fanfare, but internally triumphant. I had a turnaround of a few weeks before I headed to India for a month and there was a lot to do. I busied myself with the logistics of moving to Ireland: flights, new clothes and a business loan. I had no money, nothing to show financially for five years of dedication in Japan, so I made an appointment with the local HSBC, my bank since the age of eleven. I met the manager and showed her how I was proposing to become rich. I just needed £10,000 to get going. She looked across the desk like a stern mother. At one point I was berated for cracking my knuckles whilst describing my unique qualification in the karate world. She didn't dismiss me out of hand, but insisted that if I wanted £10,000 I would also have to deposit an equal amount into my current account. *If I had £10,000 I wouldn't be asking for it*, screamed my internal monologue.

I left the bank with thoughts that my dream might be dashed, but as soon as I got home my mum had formulated Plan B. I applied online for a six-month, interest-free EGG credit card. With no real credit history, no references, no job and no assets, they instantly approved me for a £4,000 card, which arrived three days later – cheap, instantly available money. What could possibly go wrong with a system like that? I quickly booked flights to Ireland and flew over the week after with my dad in order to meet the group there and finalize arrangements for setting up the JKS in Ireland. For such a long time this had been my plan, my dream. I was desperate to live in an English-speaking country, in a city I could walk around in, in a community that cared. Plus, it was a virgin market. For decades the Irish karate world had been marginalized and subjugated by English-based groups and instructors, and I thought I could make a difference.

JKA Ireland was a small group headed by a 4th dan called Seamus. Seamus was in his sixties; he was funny, charismatic and engaging, and had been involved in karate from the early days when martial arts had exploded into the Western world. He was bald, with a curtain of long hair at the back that was often plaited, and although not as agile as he once was, he was well respected within the group and his opinion held weight. He taught at the main dojo and the group consisted of one other dojo in Dublin, two more in the Midlands and one in Wexford. My dad and I arrived and were collected by Gayle, the organization secretary and a good friend of mine. She was in her early fifties but several years earlier had made a radical change in her life, leaving her husband and starting a Ph.D. in philosophy. Fiercely intelligent, she seemed to challenge every thought you had and I loved her company. Gayle was graciously putting us up for the few days. The meeting was held at Murphy's, a great traditional pub just down the road from her house in Rathmines in south Dublin. My dad excused himself and wandered into town while I set about getting them to approve my proposal. It was very simple: I would become technical director of JKS Ireland, Seamus would be chairman and Gayle would be secretary. However, as the only professional instructor I would be responsible for all the administration of the group. We agreed on a membership charge for students, but I insisted that dojos could affiliate for free (the dojo affiliation fee was a con). I also insisted that there would be no chief instructor; I would lead the group technically, but otherwise we would be leaders amongst equals. My new comrades seemed to accept my ideas enthusiastically as I explained the need to find a third way.

For decades there had been two choices: either join a Japan-based organization, which tended to have high standards, were legitimate but inclined to be top heavy with rules and draconian in their approach; or join a western-based group and enjoy a more *laissez-faire* attitude to regulations, sacrificing legitimacy and standards in the process. There had to be an alternative. I wanted to create a sustainable group that had the legitimacy of traditional Japanese karate, with the administrative ethos of the West. As leaders amongst equals, we would respect the journey of our colleagues whilst offering guidance along the way. I knew the time was right for a group offering the third way. However, when I came to talk about finances, Seamus started to get twitchy. I had estimated what income the group would achieve based on having a thousand members. This was my target and I saw it as being very achievable. With everyone paying for yearly membership and grading on average one and a half times per year, there would be an annual income of €21,000. I asked for a salary of €10,000 as payment for my administrative duties. Seamus seemed doubtful that I would achieve that goal, but Gayle was positive and saw it as very doable. After several pots-of-tea-worth of negotiations, Seamus eventually agreed that if I achieved the levels of membership I was talking about then I could be reimbursed for my work at a rate of €10,000 per thousand students affiliated to the group. I would also take over as squad coach and start to build my own student base within south Dublin. Seamus agreed to everything, Gayle took the minutes to distribute throughout the existing membership, and we set a date for the beginning of October, when I would move over and begin the journey.

Seamus left, my dad arrived back from being lost in Dublin and Gayle drove us up to Johnny Fox's, Ireland's highest pub, located in the Wicklow Mountains. For a Friday afternoon, thirty minutes' drive from the city centre, the pub was packed, and we soon got into the swing of things. We sat next to a roaring fire as my dad told stories of going to school with Paul McCartney, selling a box of junk to John Lennon and how his best mate 'knew' Cilla Black when she was still called Cilla White. It was fun, personal and warm, a far cry from what Japan had been, and it was what I had been longing for all these desperate years. Gayle was hilarious: she gave the appearance of blundering through life, but was, in fact, setting logical thought traps that would bite you in the arse as soon the conversation turned into a debate, which it inevitably did. It was fun and challenging. My dad, on the other hand, eased into his stride. Having been a publican for the majority of his life, I never really had the 'going down the pub for a pint with your dad' experience that so many of my friends have talked about, and this was my one chance. It was like Terry Wogan had returned to the Emerald Isle as he sat in an armchair and reminisced as the fire twinkled in his eye – such fun, and if this was the way life was in Ireland, what a choice I had made.

A week later I made my way to Heathrow to meet Dharmavira and board a plane to Mumbai. Dharmavira was a Buddhist priest with the Western Buddhist Order based in Cambridge. He was also a 4th dan at karate, a former member of the Scottish National Team, and his real name was Brian Duff. Six months earlier when Sueki and I toured the UK, we had taught at Dharmavira's dojo. He was a wonderful, sweet guy, excellent at karate and with a character you just wanted to get to know. In spite of a tumultuous past, he presented a calm exterior, an otherworldliness that comes from hours of daily meditation. Waters ran deep within him and I got the distinct impression that those waters were often turbulent. He intrigued me, and when he suggested that I accompany him on a trip to India for a month and teach karate for free to former members of the untouchables who had converted to Buddhism in order to pull themselves out of the strict caste system, how could I refuse?

We travelled through the night and arrived in Mumbai as it started to waken. A month earlier I had been in New York, the city that never sleeps. Mumbai was different: it did sleep, and most of the people slept on the roadside. As we travelled from the airport to the train station at the centre of that 13-million-people megacity, everywhere I looked people were asleep on the sides of the roads, in their rickshaws, under trees, in open doorways – these weren't homeless people in the Western sense, this was how people lived in Mumbai. We approached the train station just as the madness was beginning. People seemed to be flooding from everywhere – it wasn't rush hour like I knew it in Tokyo, with everyone generally going in the same direction. Here, chaos splintered in tangent directions everywhere I looked. Dharmavira dragged me to one side of the concourse and made his way towards a guy with a hotplate strapped to his bike. 'Fancy an omelette?' he asked.

The chap attending the bicycle sprang into action. He cracked a couple of eggs, gave them a whisk, added various ingredients and within minutes produced the goods. Filth was everywhere. I looked at the food being offered and instantly felt ill. Dharmavira insisted all was fine, and I convinced myself that nothing could go wrong with a sealed egg and a hotplate that had been scrubbed down before my eyes and heated to a temperature guaranteed to kill nasty bugs. In a real-life example of diffusion of responsibility, I tucked into my omelette. Of course, I was fine. I trusted in Dharmavira's judgment. He had spent six months a year for the last decade travelling India and teaching karate to Bushindo, a karate organization existing exclusively within the Western Buddhist Order. Boasting over 2,000 karate members, I was about to have a whirlwind tour of their major dojos and meet the senior grades of the group.

We made our way to the ticket office, purchased our first-class seats whilst seemingly taking part in the local rugby team's scrum practice and then escaped to the platform, boarded our carriage and prepared for our overnight journey to Nagpur. We sat on wooden benches with identical benches above our heads that acted as stowage. Cushions were found and the train started to creep forward. I pondered how I could broach the subject of when we would be moving to the first-class carriage, but something held me back. As we embarked we passed similar compartments crammed with travellers; at least we had this whole space to ourselves – maybe first class was just standard class but with the remaining empty seats purchased as well. I kept quiet – at least the sleeping quarters should be better.

The train rolled on and I sat back and dozed. I felt I had been travelling since July. I hadn't sat still for months, allowing all the nervous energy built up in Japan to safely leave my body. In fact for the last decade I had had a plan, a direction forward, various three-, four- and five-year strategies, and never had I deviated from them. Now as I sat on a train in India as it slowly meandered inches past family homes made from corrugated steel and corrugated cardboard, I had nothing to do but relax. I had rapidly learnt that Dharmavira's otherworldliness was part spiritual and part absent-mindedness – whether that was deliberate or not, the jury was out. Plans were vague and elusive, but living with ambiguity was not something I was used to. However, I'm a firm believer that when I am ready to learn a lesson, that lesson will be presented to me, and this train was it.

My dozing soon shifted gear to deep sleep as the jet lag kicked in. With the whole bench to myself, I settled down. Then I heard him.

'Get up!' screamed Yumoto Sensei.

'*Osu*!' I obeyed immediately as his eyes bored into me.

'What are you doing? Attack properly!' he said as he wielded the *shinai*[1]. I complied at once and paired up with a faceless Teikyo student. 'No, you stupid arsehole. In! More! *BAKA*!' He lifted the *shinai* and brought it down with a mighty thud.

I woke bolt upright, beads of sweat trickling down the back of my neck. Dharmavira looked over, making sure I was okay. Once reassured, he returned to his book. I lay back down, closed my eyes and pretended I was okay. My mind raced. I thought I had left this torment behind. Not that I knew it then, but this haunting would be part of my life for years to come, with periods of intense nightmares that made a good night's sleep impossible, followed by periods of sleep that would only lull me into a false sense of security. I didn't feel scarred by my life in Japan, in fact I thought it was normal. However, looking back, I can see the very clear connection between the ebbs and flows of life's stress and the memories of my time there. It would be something that stayed with me as long as I was connected to my sempai, although I eventually learnt to mask it. For the time being, however, I lay on the train, en route to Nagpur, and wondered exactly where I was heading.

1. *Shinai* – Japanese bamboo sword.

Later, Dharmavira and I chatted about a wide spectrum of subjects: karate in Scotland in the early days (he had been training longer than I had been alive) to the beliefs of Buddhism and benefits of meditation. Part of our trip would include a retreat where all participants would do both karate (under my guidance) and meditation (under his). The week-long event was planned for the end of our stay and I began to look forward to the meditative aspect of it.

Dharmavira ordered food from the small chap scurrying from carriage to carriage. He held a variety of ridiculously large vats of food and quickly dished up two plates of vegetable curry and a few chapatis. It was delicious and I ate quickly. Dharmavira ate with deliberate poise; there would be no seconds and over the month I learnt to savour my food. I also learnt to really enjoy vegetable curry as this would be my staple diet for lunch and dinner for my entire stay in India. Dharmavira finished and the same gentleman returned to clean away our dishes.

'Time for bed,' Dharmavira announced. I stood up to follow his lead to the sleeping carriages. He pulled his luggage from the stowage above and with a swift pull revealed a mattress, blanket and pillow. He hoisted himself up, perching as comfortably as possible on top of the ledge. I followed suit, bewildered but interested in the sudden transformation of our little compartment. There had been a neat, origami-esque pile of bedding at one end of the 'shelf' – with one pull, I produced my crib for the evening. The gentle rocking of the train soon lulled me asleep and despite my scepticism I enjoyed a deep, pleasant slumber.

The next morning I awoke to bright sunlight filtering through our window. Fully refreshed, I leapt down from my bunk and readied my belongings. After a small swill in the sink I was ready for Nagpur. We made our way from the train through the splendid colonial rail station and headed for the exit, where I could feel the heat trying to penetrate the coolness of the dark interior. Like men being released from solitary confinement, we walked through the door and into a world of technicolour. As my eyes adjusted, there in front of us were two rows of karate-*ka*, dressed in *dogi*, forming a guard of honour. I stood trying to take this in. Everywhere I looked I was dazzled by immaculately clean, bright-white *dogis*, which were only outdone by even brighter and whiter smiles.

Dharmavira moved ahead, greeting all the students, while I scurried behind. As we reached the top he stopped to shake hands with a small, slightly older guy, who was obviously the senior. I was introduced to Sadhanaratna, but struggled with the name. I had only just got used to Dharmavira slipping easily off my tongue, and realized I was going to have more difficult names to contend with. Sadhanaratna greeted me enthusiastically, and before I knew it, he was introducing me to senior members of the guard of honour, each telling me their unfathomable names as they produced garlands of flowers and placed them over my head. I was adorned with an amount of flora that would be the envy of the Chelsea Flower Show, while all the time flashes from the local press cameras added to the glare of the sun. I was a star and before I knew it, other travellers had become curious. It was my first introduction to the limited sense of personal space in India. At one point Sadhanaratna was introducing me to a young black belt, whose club I would be teaching the following day. A space-invading gentleman was standing behind my future host and despite him not wearing a *dogi*, as he had his head practically resting on the young black belt's shoulder, listening intently, I presumed he was a student. I acknowledged him and enquired to his role in the club. He looked at me strangely, shrugged his shoulders and walked off into the crowd, his curiosity obviously satisfied. What a bizarre place. We stayed a little longer in front of the grand façade of the station, Dharmavira catching up with old friends and students. They were obviously excited and Dharmavira had already explained that my presence was a fairly big deal. They had had a few British instructors teaching for Bushindo, but no one of my 'calibre'. I had experienced a moment of panic as I realized I really had to be on top form for the next month, and the greeting I received at the station only exacerbated my feelings. Thankfully, after a number of group shots had been taken, Dharmavira whisked me into a rickshaw and off we sped, destination unknown.

We whizzed past huge lorries, ornately decorated with Hindi script and colourful paint jobs. I am positive they didn't roll off the TATA assembly line in such colourful conditions, but were all lovingly created by their owners, which made it more surprising how the same loving owners drove them with such recklessness. Our rickshaw dodged and dove between these giants of the road as they hustled and bustled for contention, like some petroleum-fuelled elephant polo tournament. The only people more vulnerable than us were the motorcyclists. Several passed us with the telltale mosquito-sounding engine being revved to within an inch of their life. Many of these 125 cc machines were badly overloaded: the male driver perched on the fuel tank as his wife straddled the seat, holding on to a toddler whilst the eldest child sat side-saddle on the back, gripping on to the rear handle for dear life. No one wore helmets and I realized that in India a motorbike doubles as a family car.

After thirty minutes of running the gauntlet we made it to our accommodation: a brightly painted, manicured college that seemed to be some sort of military institution, where dazzling white curbs gave way to immaculately kept grass. We made our way through reception and were escorted to our room: an airy box with shuttered windows, a solitary rotating fan, two single mosquito-netted beds and an en-suite bathroom that only had cold water. It sounds grim, but it was in fact delightful. The shutters kept out the heat and the fan kept the cool air circulating. The cold shower was constantly used to return the core body temperature to a reasonable level and the mosquito net was all that was needed for a good night's sleep. We spent our first week there and it was heaven, a retreat from the chaos that we faced every time we left our meticulously kept environs.

After a restful night in our barracks I was treated to a tour of Nagpur. Not a city I had heard of before my trip, it was the geographical centre of India and fairly famous if you are a lover of cricket, a sport that English and Indians enjoy with equal measure whilst resenting their colonial rivals with equal enthusiasm. But my band of merry Buddhists weren't into old colonial rivalries – they had other devotions. The highlight of the day was my tour of Diksha Bhumi from a senior member from the order. This was the largest stupa in Asia and the location where Dr Ambedkar (the architect of the Indian Constitution) converted to Buddhism, along with half a million ex-untouchables, starting the resurgence of the religion on the subcontinent. I wandered around the fabulously peaceful monument as my guide oozed excitement, explaining that I was standing in the very spot Dr Ambedkar had once stood.

Outside, the conurbation of Nagpur blanketed the landscape. Roads, like tarmac tentacles, spread out from the modern city hub, facilitating a mass of construction to ooze forth. Between the arteries of modern roads were dirt tracks, alleys and back streets with buildings of varying quality filling in the blanks. It was in such stark contrast to the oasis that was Diksha Bhumi, where we walked barefoot on the cool and immaculate marble flooring. Outside, everything swirled with dust, noise and madness. After we left the sanctuary of still, tranquil air, we pottered around a few shopping areas and grabbed a bit of vegetarian lunch before setting off home, dodging lorries and cows with equal trepidation.

I was there to teach, so after a quick cold shower I changed into my *dogi* and made my way down to the waiting rickshaw. Apparently, the karate club trained at the local sports centre, so when Dharmavira and I arrived at a massive football stadium I was quite impressed. People thronged everywhere as there was some local pop-up market surrounding the entrance – how on trend, I thought. Two white guys jumping out of a rickshaw dressed in even whiter karate suits with black belts around their waist was something of interest and before I knew it the 'space invaders' had flocked. Dharmavira was having none of it and with a shove of his very strong arm I was catapulted through the crowd with a sneaky suspicion that one poor chap had been thrown to the ground. I didn't look back to confirm my suspicion, instead, I spotted the entrance of the stadium and marched on.

The entrance was dark. It was dark because it was a tunnel. I saw the light at the far end, so followed the energetically striding Dharmavira, emerging several moments later to a dimly lit football pitch.

'So where's the dojo?' I asked, still not having learnt not to ask stupid questions.

'I think they normally train on the left wing,' Dharmavira replied, with no hint of humour. We made our way over and sure enough, as we drew closer, there were about twenty students warming up in the dirt, bare-footed, with clean and ironed *dogis* looking impossibly perfect considering our present environment. Well, when in Rome – I called the class to attention and taught my first session in India.

Teaching at a local dojo in Nagpur, India, September 2002.

The guys were great; keen does not come close to describing their attitude. Like sponges they absorbed everything I said and even small, throwaway comments that I made about a technical point would be seized upon and questions were asked. It was fantastic. Their level wasn't great, but it wasn't bad. They had obviously had great instruction from Dharmavira, but it was somewhat stuck in the 1970s-style of karate that was so prevalent in the UK. Dharmavira had given them a great foundation, but understandably taught them a style of karate that hadn't developed in line with what had been happening in Japan. My job was very easy. I was teaching young, strong, keen karate-*ka* who had a solid grasp of basic karate, and all I had to do for the next month was refine them technically.

Two hours later immaculate *dogis* had given way to sweaty suits that had dusty footprints all over them as the *kumite*[2] part of the class had involved a lot of kicking. I tried to stay clean, but the students had wholeheartedly flung themselves about without a care in the world. If my sempai could see me now! It was such a far cry from Japan, where the cleaning and presentation of the dojo was as important at the training; where the Zen-like nature of the process was in itself as rigorous as the kicking and punching. However, these Buddhists weren't following the way of Zen: they may have been practising karate whilst devoting themselves to an ancient eastern philosophy, but the outcome was different. Both my sempai in Japan and these ex-untouchables had studied with a shared ancestor, but somewhere along the evolutionary tree, a new branch had been formed. Gung-ho, enthusiastic and happy, they were a pleasure to teach.

After training had finished, the young chap I had met the previous day approached me. I recognized him, despite not having a complete stranger perched on his shoulder. I complimented him on his club as he enthusiastically invited me for tea at his house – how could I say no? Twenty minutes later a rickshaw dropped us off at the edge of a shanty town. The instructor waited formally at what seemed to be a small alleyway, but was, in fact, the main entrance to the mini city.

'I live about five minutes in,' he said, gesturing us to

2. *Kumite* – the sparring element of karate.

follow. We followed – over open sewers, under live wires, past open doors and through enclosed communal areas. It was everything I expected a shanty town to be, although I never expected to feel that intangible quality of community. These people were poor, but they weren't impoverished. It didn't feel dangerous, in fact it felt the opposite.

Five minutes turned into ten as we were led through this labyrinth. Eventually we arrived at his shack. He opened the door and gestured for us to enter. Standing to attention, his wife enthusiastically gestured for Dharmavira and myself to sit on the solitary sofa, which had been covered with a well-pressed sheet. Mrs Karate Instructor didn't speak English, so she scurried through the other door and I could hear her start to make tea.

Dharmavira started the conversation by saying how he had known Sunil (thank God, I now knew his name) since he was a kid. Sunil told me how long he had been training, how he loved everything karate-related and how he had loved the class I had just taught. Occasionally I caught a glimpse of a pair of eyes edge around the door frame, followed by Mrs Sunil berating the owner of the eyes. This was then followed by the giggling of two, if not three, children.

The tea arrived, a sweet, milky drink that I sipped, smiling through gritted teeth – something else eastern that had evolved at tangents in India and Japan. However, the main event was a packet of chocolate Bourbons, so I lashed into them whilst resisting the urge to dunk. Sunil and Mrs Sunil sat, drinking and eating nothing. Everything was for us and I started to figure out this wasn't a big deal for them, this was everything. She had been in the kitchen where the unspecified number of children still sat quietly. This family home consisted of two rooms, a kitchen and this living space.

Dharmavira and I must be sitting on the family bed and I tried to pictured how maybe five people could live in such cramped circumstances. I quickly pulled my hand back from the fourth Bourbon and relished the hot tea that had been given so generously. After a few hours of them sharing their lives with us, we left these wonderful, delightful people and made our way back to a waiting rickshaw. Forty-eight hours in India, it seemed like a lifetime – the perfect city break!

When I was young the school holidays had stretched out in front of me like an eternity. Six weeks seemed like a lifetime and when I eventually made it back to school everything was new, even my best friends had radically changed, had become other in the massive gap of time since I'd last seen them. Billy Connolly has a gag about how his life is just a steady procession of hearing 'Auld Lang Syne', rapidly followed by 'Happy Birthday', then a quick leap to 'Jingle Bells' as his years whip by with shocking ferocity. Our perception of time changes as we get older, not for any biological reason, simply because our minds perceive time slower when we are experiencing new things. Like the cliché of time slowing down when you are in a car crash, in reality your mind accelerates to cope with the sudden influx of new, unexpected stimuli – so much so, that some car-crash survivors have reported only seeing in black and white as the mind abandons the capacity to absorb colour as a necessary survival mechanism to process more important stimuli. For me, this was India. Days inched by at a glacial pace, but not in a 'waiting for the working day to finish' type of way, but in a 'Jesus, I can't believe it's only midday, it seems I've been up for ages' sort of way. I enjoyed every minute. The training was great, surrounded by keen, enthusiastic karate-*ka* willing to throw themselves into everything I asked of them.

However, the added dimension was their happiness.

How strange for this to even be a consideration when we think about something that is essentially a hobby. For five years I had been surrounded by talented, dedicated karate-*ka* who had, on the whole, been unhappy. Teikyo University and the subsequent entry onto the Instructors' Course was never a path to happiness, more a feat of endurance, a rite of passage that many, including myself, felt they had to do, compelled beyond any sense of reasonableness. Here was different. Maybe it was the Buddhist learning, maybe this was just the norm. Either way, the lifetime that I spent in India was the perfect re-introduction to karate. My trip across the States had been my way of slowly moving back to the West, as I left the East behind (although the more geographical amongst you will know how directionally wrong I am there). However, India was proving to be the perfect antidote to the intense karate crucible of the Instructors' Course.

By the beginning of the fourth week we made our way to the Bhaja Retreat Centre in Pune. Seventy, maybe eighty, members of Bushindo joined us in the retreat to take part in our week-long *gasshuku*[3]. As promised, Dharmavira would be teaching me and leading everyone else through daily meditation practice, whilst I would be taking care of the more physical aspect of our regime. Twice-daily karate followed by meditation would be our strict schedule for the final week and I looked forward to being in one location for an extended period, rather than the travel that had dictated so much of our trip thus far. Life was so much slower here – slower, of course, than Tokyo and New York; slower than rural Yorkshire, where I had grown up. It was ingrained. It was expected. It was natural. My new friends had a habit of moving their heads

3. *Gasshuku* – Training camp, a coming together under one roof.

from side to side, as if their neck was some sort of slide rule. It was neither a nod of affirmation nor a shake of negativity. It was an ambiguous answer that could be implemented on an infinite number of occasions. I've seen the movement lampooned numerous times, but comedians and sitcoms miss the point. Their lateral movement of their head expresses their reality: 'yeah, maybe'. The truth was that in this reality nothing was urgent, nothing was set, nothing was 'yes' or 'no'.

The retreat, as expected, was basic, with a multi-purpose, immaculately white marble-laden hall as the centrepiece of the complex. Morning and evening I would make my way from the simple room, which I shared with Dharmavira, to the centre. Ninety minutes of karate would be followed by thirty minutes of meditation. After spending nearly every waking moment with this man for the last month, Dharmavira suddenly revealed a whole new level, a whole new depth. He led us through the process of clearing our minds, guiding us to calmness whilst allowing us to forgive the occasional intrusion of unwanted thoughts – although I suspect the guided process of the session was solely for me; my fellow meditators were well versed in the process of enlightenment. Halfway through the retreat (and I believe as a direct result of the meditation) I had a surge of energy. I wanted to push myself like I had in Japan. I sidled up to Dharmavira. 'Just keep going in this class,' I pre-emptively encouraged him. 'We will only train for an hour.' He looked at me quizzically, but accepted my comment and lined up.

'Okay! Today,' I explained to the class, 'we will do the same sort of training as on the Instructors' Course in Japan'. Grins all round. I think they expected the inner secrets. Maybe after nearly a month under my tuition I had decided it was time I shared with them the deeper knowledge

'Make a circle,' I instructed. 'Left leg forward, *gedan barai* (downwards block).' Everyone dived forward with a downward block, giving an excited *kiai* (spirited shout) in anticipation of the class. '*Gyaku Zuki* (reverse punch)!' I looked around the circle, counting the first ten senior grades. 'You guys count ten each.' They looked at each other, but I interrupted them with a '*Hajime* (start)!' They began and I quickly felt my body snap into action. As the count fell into a nice rhythm, my punches snapped out with ease. We finished our set, I changed sides and signalled for the next in the circle to continue. They did and we started the hundred with our left side.

'*Yame*.' Everyone came back to a relaxed position. I recovered quickly – my fitness seemed to be better than even during my time in Japan. 'Okay, the same with *Mae Geri* (front kick).' We stepped forward and started the sets with our right and then left legs. My kicks whipped out without aches, pains, bruises or stress. I enjoyed the process of pushing myself through the basics. It was delightful. We did the same thing with a one-two punch combination and then a similar drill with a single and double side kick. With the ease of my technique, I felt like I had imagined my sempai had felt during the instructors' training back in Tokyo.

At one point one of the young guys messed up the count. He stuttered or stumbled and broke the rhythm I was enjoying so much. Instinctively I snapped. 'Pay attention! Count properly!' Before I had time to look I caught the eye of the teenager, sweat dripping from every pore. He looked deflated. I scanned the circle and realized everyone was in the same sweaty mess. '*Yame*,' I called, embarrassed by my outburst. They all took a thankful step back to the relaxed position. I explained the importance of rhythm and pace when training like this. We were going to continue for the next hour or so and they needed to relax into the drills, rather than fighting every technique, wasting vital energy on unnecessary movement. This was the essence of the Instructors' Course – to produce a virtual wind tunnel of training to blow away all those useless, inefficient bad habits. I saw a few sideways glances as the students realized that the 'secret' of Japanese karate wasn't quite what they expected. I gave them a little time as I rearranged the class into several straight lines, then we started *Idou Kihon*, moving forward and back across the dojo, practising various kicks, punches and blocks. Sets of twenty were followed by no more than thirty seconds of rest before we would set off with a different combination. I enjoyed the flow of my movement; I was on air as I skimmed across the marble floor of the dojo. I felt completely connected to my centre, moving from my core and finishing each attack or defence with a sudden, energy-producing whip – I was definitely in the groove and felt great. I wasn't giving any instruction, hoping that the previous month's worth of classes was enough for them to focus on right now – but really, I was just being selfish, enjoying my own training too much to break the flow to teach.

We moved onto sparring, first with basic pre-arranged sets, drilling up and down the floor, then moving onto the freer sparring. My body continued to do everything I asked of it. A few times some of the students would anxiously mess up, but I had learnt from my outburst before and kept calm, not letting their actions affect my pace. We finished with *kata* and I could hear the small sighs of relief from the class as they knew the end was in sight. I was tired, too, but could still feel my blocks ping out as we went through *Bassai-dai*[4]. After a few more repetitions it was time to call it a day. I lined

4. *Bassai-dai* – a very old *kata* that most perform to achieve black belt.

them up, finished with a formal kneeling bow and dismissed the class. All I could see around me were fatigued, sweat-sodden karate-*ka*. Maybe I had pushed them too hard. Maybe this type of karate wasn't for them.

Sadhanaratna came over. I was ready to be chastised. 'Brilliant, brilliant!' He slapped me on the back and stumbled off. Two or three others followed and shared similar, albeit monosyllabic, sentiments. The guys filed out of the dojo, all smiling, all ecstatic with their accomplishment.

Two days later the *gasshuku* drew to an end, as did my time in India. Dharmavira had scheduled one day of rest before we set off home. As a treat, we would head into the mountains for a hike to the local beauty spot. I hadn't hiked since my last *gasshuku* with Teikyo University two years ago, so with delight we set off early on the last day of our month-long adventure. Guided by a few of the local senior grades, we walked through the tropical forest that surrounded the retreat. It was hot and humid, made worse by the fact that we were no longer comforted by the cool white marble of the dojo; instead we were enclosed by a thick canopy of trees, which refused to allow any air in or moisture out. Halfway up, we stumbled across a guy with a bunch of lemons.

'Do you fancy a lemonade?' Dharmavira offered.

'Of course!' Although we had brought water, some lemonade wouldn't go amiss. However, I was still edgy when it came to drinking in India. I had heard horror stories about water borne diseases and as a result had been very careful with what I drank. However, the roadside vendor set about squeezing fresh lemons into a clean glass, added some sugar and then opened a fresh bottle from the local, trusted water company. With a quick shake and stir, he presented me with the sweetest, most refreshing lemonade possible. It set me up delightfully for the second half of the climb.

An hour or so later we reached the top. It was an old fort, built hundreds of years before by the local king in defence of his land. We had a quick wander around, but with the mass of undergrowth and general unkemptness, it wasn't quite up to the British National Trust standards.

Swimming in a man-made reservoir at an abandoned fort in the hills of Pune, September 2002.

'Over here!' Sadhanaratna called from the top of a small mound. We walked over as our guides started to strip off. Our stroll quickened as we wondered what the hell was going on. As we approached the slight incline, we realized there were four enormous pools dug into the hill. Two of our guides were already cooling off, doing laps, whilst Sadhanaratna trod water, explaining that these giant, ancient swimming pools were actually hand-carved into the land as reservoirs for the fort. Still in perfect working order, they were filled with crystal-clear, very cool and terribly inviting water. I pulled off my clothes and dived in – we never had this at Teikyo!

In fact my week on the Bushindo *gasshuku* and my week on the Teikyo *gasshuku* were poles apart. Superficially they were the same: eating, training and hiking in the mountains with a group of hard-core young men and women. Eating, sleeping and sharing our lives in the true sense of what *gasshuku* means – 'together, under one roof'. But what a difference: in Japan I had felt desperately alone and longed to escape; in India I felt alive, connected. In fact I had finally rediscovered my love of karate, so far from the place where I had honed my skills.

Several hours later we made our way back to the retreat, where we would have to pack and say goodbye to India. We had spent far longer on the mountain than expected. The sun was extremely hot and after about an hour's descent our water ran out. After another hour we were getting thirsty when we stumbled across a small shack selling a milky tea. Dharmavira couldn't resist the temptation. We had forty-five minutes left of the climb, so I pushed on, leaving him to chat to the locals and drink his tea. I was thirsty, but not thirsty enough to risk the local cocktail.

I made my way back, packed, and settled into bed for one last night. Dharmavira arrived shortly after, did the same and we both enjoyed our final sleep under mosquito nets in this wonderful place.

The next day we set off early to Mumbai, made our way to the airport and flew home. Waiting for me at the airport was my mum. I felt great. A month of no alcohol, no meat and constant training had made me physically fitter and mentally healthier than I had ever been. I was also a stone lighter. Dharmavira, on the other hand, wasn't feeling so healthy. During the flight he had started to get stomach pain, and by the time we landed diarrhoea had kicked in. He spent the next few months fighting whatever bugs had been lurking in that milky drink.

THREE

Yet again I faced another quick turnaround. Bags were unpacked, clothes washed and schedules checked. I had two weeks before I flew out to Ireland in a rather permanent way. However, just after I got back home another email from Tor popped into my inbox. Although she lived and worked in Bristol, she would be spending the whole of the following week in Liverpool. She knew it was my home town and wondered if I fancied a trip over. Train tickets were rapidly booked and with the excuse of wanting to visit my Aunty Joan, I took the Trans-Pennine Express.

I never did get a chance to visit my aunty; thankfully I had failed to mention that I would be in town, therefore avoiding disappointment. Tor and I had known each other since we were nineteen, but had spent our twenties practising our relationship skills with others. Now, a decade later, we were finally together. She dropped me off at the train station the following day.

'By the way, I move to Dublin next week,' I dropped into the conversation.

'Yeah, I know,' she replied. Best deal with that little issue on another occasion then. Two hours later I met my mum in York for lunch.

'So what did Tor want?' she asked.

'Well … you know,' I shrugged.

'Yes, I do know,' came the reply.

*

The following week I stood at the top of O'Connell Street with two bags packed to bursting. Gayle had asked me to call when I was in the city centre, so I found a payphone and rang. No answer. I waited five minutes and called again, still no answer. I knew she lived on the southside, so I wandered over O'Connell Bridge and made my way towards Grafton Street.

Dublin was fantastic. For a time the second city of the British Empire, it was obviously built on merchant wealth. As I passed Temple Bar, I had the headquarters of the Bank of Ireland on my right and the magnificent Trinity College on my left, one of the oldest universities in the world, dating back to 1592. They faced each other like architectural rivals, each trying to outdo one another with ornate masonry and wrought-iron railings. I glanced through the doors of the public entrance of the bank and saw a huge open fire blazing away with a stream of customers warming themselves before they faced this particularly cold October day – the Bank of Ireland definitely won this little architectural war. The site was originally the seat of the Viking Parliament and the building had been constructed as the world's first two-chamber assembly for the Irish Government. It towered over Dame Street and oozed confidence with its Ionic columns and as I stumbled past, vagabond-esque, I couldn't help but feel at home.

I headed to Grafton Street, but actually found myself on George's Street, which I didn't know, so tried Gayle one more time.

'Hello,' came the answer. 'Oh, you're here. Right. Okay. I'll leave now.'

'You don't know where I am!' I managed to get in, avoiding her hanging up on me. I gave a brief description of my whereabouts and thankfully within five minutes she was honking her horn and causing traffic to stop just in front of where I stood. Bags were thrown into the back and I clambered aboard her rather tired-looking Opel. Five minutes later, we were back at her three-storey townhouse in the heart of the fashionable Dublin 6.

Ireland didn't have postal or zip codes like the UK or America. It was too small: postmen literally knew everyone on their round, so there was no need for that added layer of recognition. But Dublin was growing and so numbers were allocated to areas. All the odd numbers were on the northside and all the even numbers were on the southside. The odds were generally poorer than the evens and Dublin 4 and 6 were the epicentre of South Dublin wealth. I thankfully found myself slap bang in the middle of it all.

Gayle's house was a perfect example of the Regency townhouses that are ubiquitous on both the north and south sides of the city. Entering up some heavy-duty steps, which lead to the second floor, it was the quintessential upstairs-downstairs. The hall had elegant, original moulding and the ornate staircase was also of the period. To the right were a large living room and dining room. The house was divided into kitchen, my bedroom (the former servants' quarters), bathroom and pantry downstairs and two main bedrooms and an attic area upstairs. The back garden could be entered by a small landing in between the first and second floor. This home was exquisite and a far cry from what I had been used to in Japan – it was also mad. Gayle had two crazy dogs and a teenage son, David. On top of this, she was in the throes of Ph.D. hell. David was your typical teenager, into music, sport and all things hormonal. Books, magazines and papers littered every room. Gayle would flick seamlessly from *Philosophy*

Now to *The National Enquirer*, whilst David would skim through the latest heavy metal magazine whilst mastering classical cello. At the same time the dogs scampered inside and out. Judy, a nervous terrier, would chase her tail until she actually bit it and then continue the chase, spraying blood around her immediate vicinity, leaving a *CSI Miami* crime scene in her wake. Buddy, on the other hand, was the bold one: he would take to barking endlessly in the back garden as a variety of birds dared encroach on his turf. Remarkably, he even took to climbing one of the trees in the garden to ward off his evil enemy. I made myself at home.

I have a very clear recollection of what I did during those first couple of months. Years later Gayle admitted how she had worried because I had been working so hard, but at the time I had a plan and one chance to make it happen. I set about contacting every school, gym and Gaelic Athletic Association (GAA) club to see if they had any halls for hire.

It was 2002 and Dublin was booming. The city's population had only broken the million-people mark a few years before, but by the end of the decade it would have grown by 20 per cent. I arrived, like many others, at a time when real estate was going through the roof and every part of the community was under pressure. Added to this was the general provision of sports facilities in Ireland, or lack thereof. I was used to the UK, where state-funded sports centres were the norm. In Malton, North Yorkshire, where I grew up, there was an adjoining town of equal small size, separated by the River Derwent. In any other area they would have been one town, but due to historical borders of the North and East Ridings of Yorkshire, they had separate administrations. Neither could decide where to build the local sports centre, so two were built. In Japan, every ward within metropolitan Tokyo had its own sports centre, gym, martial-arts hall, swimming pool and park. It was what the government did: provide facilities for the populace. Ireland was a little different. I was told that there were actually more golf courses in Ireland than children's playgrounds. Whether true or not, I found it difficult to find prospective dojos. Gayle had told me I would struggle and not to build my hopes up – had I come over to Ireland only to find I couldn't even hire a hall?

After four weeks of constantly ringing, emailing and sending letters to a variety of establishments, I finally got a positive message – someone might have availability. I made my way to the Iveagh Gym, a private club in the heart of Dublin. They could offer me Wednesday evenings from 8.30 p.m. It wasn't ideal. Although they would allow non-members to come in to train, children would be excluded (although the time did that anyway) and an extortionate fee of €50 per hour would be charged. I took it. What choice did I have?

The next day the secretary of the local parish hall contacted me: they too had two hours on a Thursday, 6 to 8 p.m. They were cheaper, at €30 per hour. I jumped at that chance too and informed them both I would start in two weeks' time. I had no money to pay the rent, the Iveagh Gym slot was at an awful time, it was the middle of the school term so lots of children had already started activities, but I had to give it a go.

I found a newly opened stationers. Like me, they were desperate to succeed and offered cheap photocopying. I quickly designed a flyer on my ancient laptop and ordered 4,000 copies to be printed. With flyers in hand and a few A4 copies for shops I happened to pass, I began my publicity drive at the beginning of November.

When delivering leaflets, letterboxes took on characters:

some were easy to push open, others demanded you drive your hand into them like some karate spear hand strike. It was hard work and the cold didn't help, and by the time I got home each evening my fingers were numb and sore from having attacked so many advertisement-repelling letterboxes; but it worked. Each night I would return to a neatly written list of names and numbers, people who had called whilst I was out. Without an income, bank account or tax identification number, I wasn't going to get a mobile any time soon – the number on the flyer was Gayle's home number. She graciously and understandingly sat by the phone, inching her thesis towards completion whilst taking messages for me. Occasionally I would be home and hear David pick up.

'YES?' he would bark at the receiver as only a teenager could, enthusiastically answering the phone whilst simultaneously sounding pissed off. 'Who? Hang on!' Then, without moving the phone away or covering the mouthpiece, he would shout for me in a voice that fluctuated in pitch as puberty played its cruel joke. I would scramble to the phone and try to mitigate any bad first impression with a convivial 'Hi, this is Scott, how can I help?'

It was a hectic time, but names were taken, information imparted and directions given. I hoped all this diligence would bear fruit. Two weeks of hard work and walking the streets of Dublin led to a nervous Wednesday night at the Iveagh Gym. I had asked Gayle, Seamus and a few others to come along and lend a hand, or at least make the hall look less empty. As I wandered up the spiral steps of this labyrinthine gym, there was a small line of eight or so adults waiting patiently. I walked to the top of the stairs only to find the hall being used.

'I don't think we're allowed in,' the girl standing in front of the door, wearing a long, flowing dress, let me know in a thick French accent.

'Okay, maybe we are a bit early.' I knew full well we weren't and the class before was running over time.

'My name is Marianne, although most people call me Maz.' Maz was with a friend, who was equally inappropriately dressed in a long skirt. However, I was desperate to make this night a success and build student numbers.

'You're very welcome,' I insisted and then continued my greeting along the line and down the stairs to the now ten or so beginners that had turned up. Ten minutes after time the fitness class appeared to have finished, so we walked in and I spoke to the instructor, telling her we were supposed to start at 8.30 p.m.,

'Yeah, right,' came her response. I was amazed at her ability to make those two positive words sound so negative.

The class quickly started. I taught straight punch, front kick and raising block. Simple, clear, friendly and welcoming. Love me, love me, love me! I needed the students, I needed the money, I needed a dojo. They were all good guys. Except Maz and her friend, the rest were men: some young, fit guys who were obviously keen members of the gym, others who were a little older and maybe there as a result of the leaflet drop. They seemed to enjoy the class. Each paid €8.50, which was €85 for an hour's work. The hall was €50, so I had made my first bit of money in Ireland. One hour paid for a third of my week's rent! I had two more hours the following day and hoped that I would finish my first week without being in deficit.

The next day I made my way to the parish hall around the corner and got myself ready for the kids' class. It was a quarter to six. At ten to, no one was there. Eight minutes to, still no one. At seven minutes to, one girl walked through the door, followed by her mum. I remember feeling that little Victoria must be a lucky omen as she shared the same name as Tor – despite leaving Japan, I hadn't entirely given up relying on 'magical thinking' when stress levels were high. Her mum asked a few questions and I gave her a handout for the dojo. She seemed happy and turned to Victoria to wish her luck. As I took my focus away from the mum to gaze longingly at the door again I was confronted with a line of people. They had ninja-ed their way in whilst my back was turned. I greeted the next twin set of parent and child as I gave out info and assured them that their child would be safe in my custody for an hour. Successive parents paid and left their children and by five past six I had fifteen kids lined up and over €100 in my little tin. I taught a fun version of the class I had done the night before. They seemed enthused by the lesson and bounded out an hour later to happy mothers and fathers. As they did, a trickle of adults came in. Again, slowly at first, but by five past seven, I had eight adults lined up. I was off. Three hours teaching in two venues over two days. Total overheads: €110. Total takings: €265. That was it! I was a professional instructor. After paying Gayle rent, I still had enough money in my pocket to contribute to my share of the food bill and a few pints. I was all set. Six weeks and 4,000 leaflets was all it had taken to make the most important step of my life.

Of course, teaching karate was only one aspect of my professional career. I had to be good at it as well. Since leaving Japan three months ago I hadn't been training properly. Sure, my time in India had been physically tough. A few hard sessions and a strict diet had made me fit and strong. Even my time in America had trimmed me up as I had only been able to afford two meals per day. However, I also needed to be good at karate, not just thin enough to do it. When I first moved in with Gayle I had asked her where I could go jogging. Directions to the River Dodder were given. It was very simple: 'Down there, turn left. You can't miss it.' I had set off, gone down and left but failed to see a stream, let alone a river. I jogged and jogged until my normally good sense of direction failed me. After about an hour, sweating profusely, I stopped a lady who looked like she needed a rest from carrying her bags of shopping.

'Excuse me,' I tried not to pant. 'Do you know how I can get to Rathmines from here?'

'Are you driving?'

'No,' I said as I wiped sweat from my drenched face. 'Running.'

'Oh,' she said with a pained look on her face. I didn't think I had gone that far, but the thirty-minute run home proved otherwise.

I had to find a way to train. Seamus, the fatherly chairman of our group, had a dojo close to Gayle's. Gayle hadn't been training regularly as her Ph.D. sucked up every ounce of time and energy, but she did offer to drop me to the dojo at the appropriate time. So, *dogi* in hand, I made my way to training. The class was small, but Ian, a young instructor from the Midlands and one of his top students, and a middle-aged, friendly brown belt called Jack, had also turned up. There were one or two other colour belts, but that was it. Seamus was pleased to see me and I was pleased to be stretching and moving once more.

I had known Seamus since university. Thirty-five years my senior, he was one of those stalwarts you can find in any organization, having seen and done everything, conveying his wisdom as and when he saw fit. I remember the first time he had invited me to teach at his dojo. Whilst at university, Noel, a senior from the group who lived in the Midlands, had invited me to teach for the weekend. On the back of that, Seamus had asked me to teach his regular class on the Monday. In those days, I would have taught for beer money, so to be invited to teach in Ireland, be looked after, fed, watered and paid, was a true delight. Seamus had been funny and eccentric, and was one of those guys you often find in northern British cities (and obviously Ireland too). He was fiercely working class, but self-educated and clever. Witty and artistic, his ponytail spoke of an eccentric side that was reinforced by the customized paint job on his Fiat Panda: it looked like a tube of toothpaste. The first time I met him he was full of praise for my class and my karate. I remember him picking up my bag, as is customary for juniors to look after one's seniors. 'Jesus, Seamus,' I said, grabbing my bag from him. 'You're old enough to be my dad!' He was a great guy, very respectful and a delight to be with.

We started training and it all changed. Whether it was because (for the first time) he was teaching and I was training; whether it was because Ian and Jack were present and he felt he had to up his game; whether it was the testosterone, I don't know. The atmosphere had changed. Seamus called out combinations, long cumbersome combinations without consistency or logic. I pinged out my techniques like someone who was eager to train hard again, but Seamus would stop the class and instruct us all to do 'his' combination in the way 'he' wanted us to do it. Naively, I didn't immediately catch on that he was actually talking about me. But before long I realized that every 'teaching point' was in opposition of what I was doing. I continued on regardless and before long Ian and Jack were glancing sideways, checking what I was doing, rather than following Seamus's lead. He was in his mid-sixties, I was twenty-nine. We were both 4th dan, but I had just spent the last five years training in Japan with Yumoto Sensei and graduated from the Instructors' Course. There was no comparison and I hoped he wasn't going to make this an issue.

The class finished. Seamus was very curt, but Ian and Jack said something about it being lovely to train with me and left with smiles on their faces. Gayle picked me up and read my face. 'So tell me all … over a pint.'

We sat in Murphy's, the very same pub where all the senior members had met and discussed me moving to Ireland. I explained the situation. There was nothing concrete to say, just a feeling, an impression. Gayle had been friends with Seamus for over twenty years, and saw the problem straight away.

'Fucking men and their fucking egos,' she blurted out whilst drinking her Guinness. I hoped she wasn't talking about me, but I knew it didn't bode well for a cooperative future, being *leaders amongst equals*. 'Well,' she concluded, 'we're going to have to watch that one'.

I never went back. What was the point? It only antagonized Seamus and the training wasn't what I was looking for. The following week, Gayle suggested we train at the university. As well as finishing her Ph.D. she was also teaching at University College Dublin. UCD was a five-minute drive from her house and as a member of the teaching staff, she could use the sporting facilities. So we started training there in the mornings. It suited Gayle, as she could then get back to the keyboard. It suited me as it got me out of bed and kickstarted my body into action, ready for a hard day chasing time slots in sports centres and delivering leaflets. By mid-November I had a regular training schedule – three classes per week – and a plan for growth.

The issue with Seamus bothered me. He had only come to my initial class at the Iveagh and not been back since. When I lived in the UK, he was the one inviting me over to teach once or twice a year. Now that I was in the same city as him, he gave me a wide berth. I also stayed clear of his classes. But squad training was scheduled for the following week. I went along believing I was supposed to teach, as that had been part of the initial agreement back in August. I turned up to find Seamus had already taken control. I was told to line up with the rest of the students and he set about teaching basic, one-step sparring. This was squad training, aimed at preparing our students for competitions. I had ideas – I had lots of ideas: how to build speed, timing and distance for competition fighting, for example, but we were all forced to focus on a rudimentary, vacuous set of drills whilst Seamus spat out 'harder, faster, stronger'. It was bizarre and when Gayle questioned him on why I wasn't teaching, he waved her away with a 'that was never the agreement'. She left, disgusted and let down.

Of course we talked. It became the hot topic over dinner and the once- or twice-weekly visit to Murphy's, until Derek (the resident barman) would sidle over with our compulsory second pint and tell us to leave this poor Seamus alone. 'Whatever he's done,' Derek would chip in, 'he can't be that bad!'

The fact of the matter was that this was not good news. I was nothing in Ireland and I needed to cooperate with these guys, and collaboration was the only way forward. I had seen the slow – and sometimes rapid – implosion of karate groups within the UK as I had come through the grades. Large national bodies had peaked and then gone into permanent decline. The groups centred around one main figure. Charismatic and talented, these solitary instructors formed associations that spread and developed around them. However, like many types of groups in many aspects of life, they had failed to see the cyclical nature of these things and before they knew it, former devoted students began to feel stifled, unappreciated and held back. People left, splits happened and former great instructors were left with nothing.

I didn't want that to happen. I knew we had set the foundations of the creation of a sustainable model, but it would only work with cooperation. I couldn't allow my ego to limit the future potential of JKS Ireland, so I bit my lip and allowed Seamus to play out his demonstration of power. He had agreed with Gayle that I would take over the squad from January, so I could wait.

Besides, I was being distracted from such troublesome matters by Tor. I left for Ireland the week after I had seen her in Liverpool, but we had quickly fallen into a pattern of speaking to each other every day. As soon as I moved over I booked a flight to Bristol for the following weekend. As I had no fixed schedule, I flew in early on the Friday morning and back early Monday morning. Tor would then reciprocate two weeks later and fly in late Friday evening, after work, and then back early Monday morning. Long-distance relationships aren't great, but this was perfect. Seeing each other twice a month may not be conducive to getting to know someone, but we had already been very good friends for a decade. Most importantly, it gave me valuable space to focus on work. I woke up every morning thinking 'how can I earn my keep today?' and I would go to bed mentally totting up what I had achieved that day in comparison to how much it had cost me to exist. Future work I had initiated to sustain me for the coming weeks was also taken into consideration. It was exhausting. That constant tallying of food eaten, rent paid, photocopying done etc., compared to work done and money earned, was all-invasive but utterly essential. I always knew how much money I had used on my credit card, how much money I had in my bank and how much was in my wallet. As I built up the three classes, I kept a record of students who trained and how much I was being paid. It was exceptional training for the future development of the group, but at the time it weighed heavily on my mind. The weekends with Tor were a welcome relief, a chance to recharge before Monday mornings when I would dive head first into work again.

But stress always finds a way out. After we had been together for a month or so, Tor broached the subject.

'You don't half twitch a lot, don't you?'

'What do you mean?' I had no idea where this conversation, first thing in the morning, was going.

'Well, when you're asleep, you twitch … well, you actually kick … maybe punch. Do you fight people in your sleep?' She had quickly found a way to ask the question she had wanted to. Apparently I had been fighting someone in my sleep. Several weeks after she first asked me, I actually punched her in the ribs whilst we both 'slept peacefully'. Luckily it was dismissed with a joke and instant forgiveness. But the stress was ever present. I often found myself sitting up on the edge of the bed, a volcano of emotion rumbling away. I would feel the *fuck you* come out of my mouth and then I would be back, grabbing onto my stomach and wondering what had happened.

Occasionally the faceless adversary gave way to Yumoto Sensei or Takahashi Sempai, but mostly they were vague and ambiguous – impossible to confront and deal with. So I battled on. I hadn't slept properly since I was a teenager, when I had bouts of insomnia, so this was no different. I could function throughout the day, that was the main thing.

Tor's visits to Ireland during 2002 were a welcome respite during those first few months in Dublin. I was settling into the city slower than anticipated, but once I came to appreciate my situation I was happy with the assimilation. Ireland, as naive and stupid as this may sound, was a foreign country. When my dad came over with me in August, I scoffed at him when I had heard him exclaim to the barman, 'What do you mean, you don't take sterling?' I realized I harboured the same prejudices, albeit a little more subtly. It is easy to convince oneself that the Irish are the same as the British: people across the world have been doing it for centuries. We share a similar language, legal system, government system, pop culture – you walk down Grafton Street and the shops are the same as any high street in the UK. It is easy to believe British and Irish people are the same, but they aren't. Subtle and intrinsic, it is only a superficial understanding that allows you to think the two cultures are equal. I set about integrating myself, just like I had done in Japan – by going out to pubs and learning the local slang.

Noel had sent me two brown-belt brothers from his dojo in the midlands. His students had started studying at UCD and after a few sessions in my dojo, arrangements for drinks had been made and I set out for my first foray into town. We didn't make it far, because apparently Rathmines was the place to be on a Thursday: a few pints in Toast followed by drinks and dancing in Tramco. I couldn't believe how packed it was. We sat in Tramco as the brothers shouted over the noise about such subtleties of use of *craic*, *feck*, *Janey Mack*, *langers*, *locked*, *your hole* and so on. So a conversation might go along the lines of, '*Janey Mack*! What great *craic* this is, the place is *black*! I'm *langers*, but you're *locked*! There is no way you're going to *get your hole* tonight, you better *feck* off home.'

I was fascinated and enthralled. I never liked nightclubs, but this place was wonderful, different from its counterparts in the UK. People were there for the *craic* rather than being there to crack someone's head open, something that is fairly prevalent in the binge-drinking culture of northern England. We stumbled to the exit at two in the morning and I noticed an elderly couple sitting in a quiet area near the door. I would never have seen such a thing in the UK: a couple in their sixties, having a late-night drink in a nightclub. Music blasted out upstairs and you could feel the thud of the thousand or so students from the three major universities of Dublin dancing away. However, this couple sat with complete ease, sipping a whiskey and a glass of wine. The fresh winter air hit us and I instantly felt hungry – ah, a chance to use my new linguistic skills.

'You look like you know where the nearest *chipper* is,' I said as I sidled up to a girl who had just left the club as well.

'I beg your pardon!' she replied rather sharply. I thought I had used the wrong idiom for a fast-food joint. I then noticed that this young lady was rather big-boned.

'I didn't mean …' There was nowhere I could go with this one.

The following weekend Tor was over. During our university days, she had trained hard and gained her black belt in the university club in a record time of three years. Having spent her childhood from the age of three until she was eighteen practising ballet, she had natural poise and body control that worked well for karate. Then, as captain of the British Ladies' Karate Team, she added a number of European titles to her name. In recent years her training had waned, but I was delighted that as we were now together her interest in karate increased once more. She had brought her *dogi*[1] and we decided that, with Gayle, the three of us would train at UCD. We arrived, Gayle parked the car, and we walked to the sports centre. As we approached, two guys were walking the other way. Tor is exceptionally good-looking, so I had become used to men gawping at her wherever we went, and these two were no different. As they approached, with perfect timing, Tor

Enjoying a night out with Gayle (left) and Tor (right), Dublin, December 2002.

commented, 'Jesus, my *gi* is really smelly. I haven't washed it in weeks.' The two gents, now directly to our left, shuddered in disbelief. Gayle was in fits of laughter and Tor looked

1. Most of the Western world refer to their karate suit as their *gi*. In Japan it is often referred to as their *keikogi* (training clothes) or *dogi* (clothes to find the way). In Ireland *dogi* is used because in Irish *gi* refers to something else. It is the most vulgar expression that can be used to refer to a lady's genitalia.

around, searching for the cause of such hilarity. She, too, had to get to grips with the lingo.

A few weeks after I opened my first dojo, I received emails from two independent dojos from the UK. They would later playfully squabble about who joined first, but if memory serves me right, Colin from Leeds made first contact, rapidly followed by Stu in Wigan. They wanted to join the JKS. I quickly put into place forms, licences and the standard organizational structure that would accommodate the JKS in both the UK and Ireland. It was fantastic news and Gayle gave me a welcome pat on the back.

'You're going to be all right,' she said, clinking my glass as we sat in Murphy's having a celebratory pint. 'All your hard work is paying off and it will be great.' She had confidence in me, which I dearly wished I shared: I was plagued by doubt and fear. Doubt about my ability to build the group – as a 29-year-old 4th dan, I felt woefully young and underqualified. Fear of my level slipping due to lack of a regular sensei, as this was the first time in my life without an instructor to follow. I also feared lack of money. I had been poor in Japan, but in Ireland I was even poorer. I was covering living costs, but that didn't include the flights back and forth to Bristol to see Tor. I checked my credit card daily, watching the amount owed nudging closer and closer to the £4,000 credit limit. Fear would intrude at regular intervals as the realization that in January the six-month, interest-free period that suckered customers into the credit system would expire. I would then have to start paying the balance off whilst servicing the debt at 17.9 per cent interest. I wouldn't be able to do that on three classes per week. But for now, sitting in Murphy's with Gayle, drinking Bulmer's cider, it was a good day.

Several days later we met Seamus at the Walkinstown

branch of the Bank of Ireland to change the organization bank account from JKA Ireland (their old group name) to the JKS. I was also to become a signatory for the group. I announced the great news that we now had two affiliated dojos in the UK.

'So maybe the account should be JKS GB & Ireland?' I suggested.

'No. JKS Ireland & GB.'

I looked at Gayle and she just shrugged her shoulders. Fight the battles you can win, she seemed to say. The name made no real difference to me, but it did to Seamus, so I let him dominate proceedings and hoped he would be happy. At least we had all the infrastructure in place to run the group and move forward.

By the beginning of December the initial surge of interest in my three classes seemed to fall. This was normal and expected, but it was hit more by most Dubliners' desire to stop everything in the run up to Christmas. As the classes were pay as you go, children and adults alike seemed to be off shopping, partying and being all things merry instead of training. I knew people hadn't quit and still liked what I was doing, but I would teach one week to half the normal class only to find the next week numbers were similar, but last week's missing 50 per cent had turned up instead. My fixed costs were set, so money was tight. Gayle was also feeling the pinch. She had decided to visit her native Australia after over two decades of living in Ireland. She would be away for several weeks over Christmas and New Year and was also on a very limited budget; the considerable costs of the holiday season being relocated to Australia had taken its financial toll.

At the start of the month we had done our weekly shop and discovered that Tesco had a huge joint of ham on special offer. We snapped it up and Gayle cooked it to perfection.

We set about gnawing our way through the joint; ham soups were made and slurped for lunches. Ham and potato cakes were the *plat du jour* for an entire week. At one point ham curry was proposed and cooked with adequate results. In fact we had very little else for the first two weeks of December. However, by the third week we had had our fill and opening the fridge to the seemingly self-replicating piece of meat was depressing. We splashed out and brought ourselves a take-away from the local Chinese. Prawns, chicken, cashew nuts, rice, spices and an assortment of vegetables made our night. It was an oasis in a desert of ham. However, the next day we had to go back to our cold meat as we had blown a substantial part of the food budget the night before. Midway through the final week of ham, it started to show signs of greenness. We didn't want to guess what it was, so we cut a large section of the meat away, like a surgeon sacrificing an infected limb to save the rest of the body. We kept on eating and didn't suffer any noticeable side effects, and at least we were feeding ourselves.

By the end of the third week of December, Gayle left for Australia and I had a few more days before Christmas. The cold weather hit Dublin and I was thankful for the thick winter coat my mum had bought me before moving over. I had no gloves or hat though, and cycling to the two dojos and various chore-related locations around the city was a painful experience. I spotted a shop with gloves for sale at €5. They were cheap, but I couldn't afford them. I needed the money for food until I got home for Christmas, so I resorted to using several pairs of socks as makeshift mittens. They did the job – and I still had the fiver in my pocket.

I finished the final few classes, even though I actually lost money as the hall rental was more than the total money taken in. I put it down to experience and hoped that in the New Year the students would be back and I would be revitalized to deliver the 5,000 leaflets I had ready for January. I jumped on a Ryanair flight ready to spend the holidays with my family and Tor.

FOUR

January 2003 was a cold one, and this was before the days when global warming made Irish winters fairly bearable. I walked up and down icy windy avenues desperately trying to deplete the pile of flyers in my bag. In later years I would use leaflet-distribution companies to deliver tens of thousands of leaflets, and I always feel sorry for the Eastern European immigrants working for minimum wage as they delivered 20–30,000 of my advertisements. It was soul and sole destroying, never-ending work, but for now I had to soldier on. Christmas had further depleted funds and I arrived back to Ireland broke. But before I left I had managed to secure two hours per week at a large secondary school, St Killian's in Clonskeagh. Ten minutes' cycle from where I lived, it was surrounded by housing estates and I had convinced myself it was the answer to my financial problems. In fact, I had convinced myself so much that I had signed a contract to take the two hours per week for the whole year. The rent was expensive at €45 per hour, but thankfully I only had to pay at the end of each term. As I signed the contract, promising to give the school nearly €3,000 in the coming year, I saw this as my salvation, not the huge burden that it could possibly become. However, in the cold, harsh light of the New Year, I realized what I had committed to, and set about trying to avoid financial ruin.

For the first two weeks of January, I re-canvassed all the areas I had covered the previous autumn and then added the housing estates surrounding St Killian's. It dawned on me that the estates around the school added an extra dimension to the ordeal. In Dublin 6, houses tended to be in terrace formation: I could walk along the road and rapidly fire flyers through the letterboxes. On odd occasions, gates and small paths were involved, but that was all. Sometimes I would come across a large townhouse, but I would eagerly stride up the steps as I knew they had been converted to flats and I could offload a dozen flyers at once.

But Dublin 14 was farther south, away from the city centre. Less crowded meant more land, meant bigger houses, meant bigger gardens and meant longer and longer garden paths. A 100 metre-long avenue meant a kilometre of walking up and down paths that meandered randomly around manicured lawns. I couldn't afford to miss them as most looked like family homes, but I also couldn't afford to run across lawns, just in case prospective students' parents were peering at me through twitching curtains. I didn't want to risk a potential 'sale'. So every morning I woke to the dread of the daily trek, had a quick breakfast, put on as many layers as possible and set out. I stopped for lunch, grabbing a sandwich and a cup of tea and then marched on again until it got dark, which was mercifully at 4 p.m. Towards the end of the week I turned a corner and walked up the avenue of the last housing estate I was going to do. I popped a flyer into the first detached house and skipped over the shared driveway to the next. By the time I got to the third, a rotund individual was bounding towards me with a face like a boiled ham and the flyer gripped tightly in his sausage hands.

'Can you not read, fecking idiot?' Calling me stupid was always a trigger, ever since my A Level history teacher called me 'semi-illiterate' and proceeded to read out a hastily written essay I had handed in.

'I beg your pardon?' I came across rather English, which didn't help the matter.

'Did you not see the fecking sign above my letterbox?' I knew the nuances of feck compared to fuck, but said aggressively, it still riled me.

'No sorry, I didn't. But maybe you would be interested?' I gestured to the flyer hoping he would see the picture of me on the front doing an impressive kick.

'I'm not interested in anything from you.' He had got rather close during this exchange and I was hoping I wouldn't be forced to create another way of advertising my new club. 'So stick this up your arse!' He tried to fling the flyer at me, but it fluttered impotently to the ground like a badly made paper aeroplane. He stormed off.

I was gobsmacked. Why was he so angry? Surely putting the flyer in the recycling bin would have been less stressful for him – and he would have been helping the environment. Maybe he was just an arsehole. Ironically, karate probably would have done him the world of good. In the following years as my career would regularly veer into the world of leaflet delivery man, I would meet many of his kind: angry men (always men), ready to vent at the world around them for no particular reason.

Back to the job at hand, I was hoping for the best but planning for the worst. In the evenings I had started to research the possibility of using my Post-Graduate Certificate of Education (PGCE) in Ireland. My PGCE allowed me to teach up to secondary school level. I had never used it and never wanted to, but I was getting desperate. I needed to start paying off the £4,000 credit card bill and if I didn't start making minimum payments, they were entitled to ask for the whole amount back at once. Besides, how long could I go without earning a subsistence level of income? I figured I may be able to do a little substitute teaching, covering for teachers who had called in sick. It was possible. My qualification was recognized in Ireland and with an income of €150 per day, it would be a lifesaver – all I needed to do was register.

However, it was the Rubicon. I knew that as soon as I passed that line I would never be able to focus solely on karate, and there would be no way back. This weighed heavily on my mind as I made an appointment to meet the agency on Tuesday 14 January. On Monday 13 January I would have the first night at the secondary school – St Killian, whoever he was, would be my last chance of salvation. I went to bed late on the Sunday evening, at the end of a weary fortnight, and hoped a good night's sleep would bring in a new week and a new start.

I woke an hour later, sitting on the side of my sofa bed, knees pushed up to my face, grabbing my stomach. It was the strangest feeling. In that nether region of a waking dream, I tried to force the energy from my body, an electrical current of base fear. Pulling my shoulders back, I opened my chest, hoping I could breathe my way to calmness. Finally I shook my head, rattling the vague images from my mind. I slumped back into bed, still half asleep. An hour later I found myself back on the edge, repeating the same midnight dance. And again. And again. A horrible, horrible night's sleep, that left me exhausted, physically and emotionally. I needed to be saved from this.

Praise be to God … and St Killian! I made my way to the school. Gayle had come for moral support and we were met by a sea of people. Nearly fifty students, a mixture of kids and adults, had turned up. Gayle diligently took training fees as I met and greeted the new students coming through the door. The hall was cavernous and cold, with a tiled floor that must have made sense to someone at some time. The venue was made worse by the fact that before us a group of footballers, not content with playing inside, had brought half a pitch in with them. Mud and grit covered every inch of the tiling, making training in bare feet like walking on sandpaper. The only positive was that the tiles were so cold it had a numbing effect on the soles, therefore mitigating the sanding effect. Through a combination of my sheer delight of the numbers, a release of adrenaline and a desperation to please, I taught a fantastic class that no one could help but be enthused by. Gayle and I left an hour later surrounded by a sea of happy faces and promises to see us again next week. We raced home and I emptied the money tin onto Gayle's kitchen table. We had taken over €300. I immediately emailed the teaching agency, cancelling my appointment: the PGCE that had weighed so heavily on me for the last few months was never thought of again.

Still euphoric, I made my way to the school the following Thursday. This class was later in the evening, so I had directed most of the adults who had enquired to this day. I had an equally impressive fifteen students, all adults and all keen to learn. Even after the rent, I still made €70 for the hour and as they were a different crew from the Monday, it meant I had increased my membership by over sixty students. The Wednesday and Thursday classes continued as before Christmas, most students had made a welcome return, plus the limited leaflet drop and word of mouth had helped to repopulate the classes, compensating for the natural drop off that happens in any club.

In February a new gym opened just over the road from Gayle's house. LA Fitness was a UK chain that was trying to make inroads into the Republic. The day it opened I went in and spoke to the manager, a young guy who was obviously new to this senior role but keen to make it his own. They had a perfect dance studio and its schedule was virtually blank. I quickly negotiated a kids' and an adults' class. The manager would allow me to invite non-members into the club and we agreed a rent of €25. He also helped promote the classes with flyers and after a week of standing in the lobby, *dogi*-clad, handing out more flyers, I was ready for my first class. The kids' class, starting at 4 p.m., was a bit of an unknown as no one was teaching karate at that time anywhere in Dublin. However, primary schools finished as early at 1:30 p.m. and Gayle was convinced parents were at a loss to know what to do with their kids in the afternoons. The class was packed – albeit packed meant twenty kids in the small studio. The following day the adult class had enticed another six or seven new adults. I had mentioned to existing members that this class was also available and I was pleased to see that Maz had encouraged, cajoled and insisted a similar number of existing members come along.

By the end of the month I had found a small venue in Stillorgan, a 45-minute bike ride from Rathmines. I could have the venue, which was able to hold no more than ten kids, any time I wanted. I fitted it into my schedule. With rent at €12 it would be quite profitable if I could fill it, but it would literally be an uphill struggle to get there.

I couldn't have hoped for a better start to 2003. The eight classes a week gave me about 130 students. Some adults trained twice or three times per week, so I was teaching about 150 students per week. On top of this, Noel had decided that he wanted to invite me to teach at his dojo in Castlepollard on a regular basis. He worked in a large business park to the west of Dublin, imaginatively called Citywest. So a plan was hatched that I would take the bus out to his office on the Friday evening. I would then travel to Castlepollard with Noel after work, spend the evening with him and his lovely family, being splendidly fed and watered. I would then teach his club on the Saturday, get my €100 daily fee and then head back to Dublin on the evening bus. If I did this twice monthly, I could still see Tor on alternate weekends and start to teach students other than white belts.

I was suddenly not only earning my keep but also managing my debt and having enough in the bank for Gayle and me to never have to worry about eating green ham again. In the spring I would add an extra kids' class in Irishtown on a Wednesday, which would make my working week complete, with a kids' and adult class every day. I had set out a goal of getting a hundred students to sustain my life and within six months I had achieved that and much more. The prospect of substitute teaching was a distant memory and I never looked back. Everything was perfect.

Well, almost. Building a professional dojo was part one of my plan. Part two was building the JKS in Ireland and the UK. It was early days, but I knew that inviting Yumoto Sensei to teach in Ireland was the key to putting us on the karate map. When I first arrived it was decided that we would invite Yumoto Sensei to Dublin in March 2003. I had contacted him and a date had been arranged. However, at the end of January I contacted him again to arrange flights. I'd called the headquarters at a time when I knew he would be free, but he came to the phone not being his normal *genki*[1] self. He

1. *Genki* – Energetic. A ubiquitous adjective in Japanese.

informed me he had to cancel the seminar.

'I promise you,' he said, 'if it were up to me, I would be there for you. I want to help you, I want the JKS to succeed, but I can't go. I am so sorry.'

'But, Sensei, what is the issue?' I was generally nervous when I spoke to Yumoto Sensei, but my stress levels had just gone through the roof as I processed all the possible consequences of this turn of events.

'Ishii Sensei and Taguchi Sensei,' he said. He didn't need to say more, but he did. He explained in minute detail. I hung up the phone and Gayle was already by my side. I explained all.

The TBKA had continued to exist as a shadow group on the periphery of the JKS. Taguchi Sensei was the Chief Instructor of both the JKS and the TBKA. All JKS instructors and affiliates were bound by official rules. Yearly membership had to be paid, dan gradings were registered in Japan and the vast majority of the fee went to the organization. Even Headquarter Instructors who were invited to international seminars had to give part of their fees back to the organization. This was all done without resentment as the money helped fund and promote the Headquarters, our World Championships and the Instructors' Course. The TBKA, on the other hand, was Taguchi Sensei's private group, and he and its members didn't play by the same rules. Taguchi Sensei's biggest supporter in the TBKA was Ishii Sensei. I had spent a long time in Japan convincing seniors of the JKS that I no longer had any connection with Ishii Sensei; in fact I was specifically asked that question when I took the test to enter the Instructors' Course. It had come back to haunt me. Taguchi Sensei had told Yumoto Sensei he could not go to Ireland at my invitation. I was Ishii Sensei's student and Ishii Sensei was the representative of the JKS/ TBKA in Ireland.

In fact Ishii Sensei did have a reasonably sized group in Ireland headed by a 6th dan in the south. This instructor was close to Ishii Sensei and Gayle later heard that he had bragged about how he had put a stop to Yumoto Sensei coming to Ireland – he and Ishii Sensei had indeed stopped one of the best instructors in the world from teaching in Ireland for the first time. I felt it was very little to be boastful about. Either way, Yumoto Sensei would not be coming to Ireland.

I explained all to Gayle, but she had an answer. Yumoto Sensei had taught in the UK in both 2001 and 2002, so why couldn't we change the seminar to the UK? I rang him back immediately.

'Yes, of course,' came the reply. 'That's it. We will do that.' And so, in the space of thirty minutes we had grasped a small victory from the jaws of defeat. It was also ironic that Taguchi Sensei could forbid Yumoto Sensei from travelling to Ireland on Ishii Sensei's request. But he couldn't do the same for the country where Ishii Sensei resided. We were off to England!

The issue was where to host the seminar. The two clubs that had joined the JKS were small, and I needed someone who had a bigger student base to help out. Peter was a sempai of mine from before I had moved to Japan. In fact we had competed regularly together as part of Ishii Sensei's national team, achieving numerous National and European titles. He was a tough guy who had fought all his life to survive and now seemed to be thriving. Peter had left Ishii Sensei's group the year before I went to Japan due to, of course, money. He had moved to Leicester from his native Scotland and set about building a strong dojo under the affiliation of Ishii Sensei.

At some point he had become tired of inviting Ishii Sensei to his dojo, as was compulsory, in order to have the three yearly *kyu*[2] gradings.

Despite having in excess of 150 students paying a grading and training fee, Ishii Sensei's bill always seemed to be higher than the money taken in, so Peter had to pay from his own pocket for the privilege. Of course, anyone from the outside world could see the unsustainability of such a system and sometime in early 1996 Peter decided that he was capable, with twenty-five years' karate experience, of grading kids up to the next colour belt level. He left the TBKA and had gone from strength to strength, creating his own independent association, boasting a fully funded squad that travelled throughout the world competing and winning at the highest level.

I had never lost touch with him and in fact had picked his brain many times when I moved to Ireland in order to get ideas about setting up my own group. He was the first and only person I called.

'Hi Peter, it's Scott.'

'What can I help you with now?'

'Actually, would you like Yumoto Sensei to teach a weekend seminar at your dojo?'

I could hear him nearly fall off his chair. Yumoto Sensei was major league. Until then, Peter had only run special, monthly classes for black and brown belts taught by himself. So to have one of the best karate sensei in the world at his dojo was a quantum leap. He accepted and would help host the event and I was glad to work with him; it was payback for all the help he had given me. The next issue was breaking the news to Seamus. A meeting was arranged at our office, Murphy's pub in Rathmines.

---

2. *Kyu* – the nine colour belts leading up to black.

'This is just typical.' Seamus was angry, a side of him I had never seen. 'You lied to us, you said the JKS was completely independent of the TBKA!' His accusation was personal. I tried to reason with him. The event in the UK was going to be hugely popular, and there was profit to be made. We could run it as a JKS Ireland & GB event and the group would benefit from the profits. Or we could run it as a JKS GB event and I would benefit from the profits.

'I'll have to have a think.' He left the pub without saying anything else. Gayle looked at me. She was at a loss. She had known Seamus for over twenty years, but she was as surprised as I was.

The next day we got a message. He wanted a meeting before the first squad training of the year scheduled for the coming Sunday.

'Well, at least he'll be at training,' I joked with Gayle. Finally I had been put in charge of the squad and we had pondered whether Seamus would show up or not. Would he train under me, something he had only done once since I moved over, when he had shown up to help on my first night at Iveagh Fitness Centre? Since then, it seems that his admiration of my karate, admiration that had led to him inviting me to Ireland regularly in the nineties, had greatly waned.

We turned up thirty minutes before training as we had been assured it 'wouldn't take long'. Seamus had summoned the whole gang. Cathal, a 2nd dan from Wicklow, was sitting at his side. Cathal had become increasingly defensive once I had moved over and set up my venues. He had been the number two of this small parochial group, but to him it was a lot. At one point he had told me that Seamus would always be the chief instructor and that, as he said, was *that*. Next to Cathal was Ian, a young guy who had taken over one of

Noel's clubs in the Midlands. He had then gone on to open another and probably had the largest number of students in the association. Cathal was angry. Ian looked bewildered – I noticed he was the only one who had a kit bag with him. Seamus tried to look presidential, sitting bolt upright, hands on knees and arms straight, hackles raised.

Normal pleasantries were abandoned. 'So, what's the *craic*?' I knew I was going to be screwed over, so I thought at least I could be nonchalant about it. But too much of my awful Irish accent came out and I just came across as a dick.

Seamus raised his shoulders even higher. 'Well, I'm out.' He stood up and swept his arm dramatically around the room. 'Who's with me?'

Cathal quickly followed suit whilst Ian looked on with amazement and Gayle seethed with a mixture of disgust and anger.

'But Seamus, what will you do?' He had nowhere to go. I knew with certainty that this would end his karate career. I also knew that the JKS was the way forward. He didn't bother answering and so ended the shortest meeting in the history of Anglo-Irish meetings. Ian looked at me, confused. I filled him in on the recent unfortunate turn of events with Yumoto Sensei. He shrugged, as only an eighteen-year-old can, and then we decided it was time to get changed and warm up. Squad training went remarkably well and we left the dojo, Seamus's dojo, and waited to see what the fallout would be.

The group split. Seamus and Cathal took their dojos to create a new group, calling themselves Traditional National Union of Karate – we preferred to reverse the acronym. Ian was at a loss to know what to do. Seamus had been part of his karate journey since he was a kid. I was new on the scene. So he made the very strange decision *not* to decide. He had two clubs, so affiliated one to the JKS and the other one to TNUK. It made me feel better that he decided to affiliate his biggest club to me, but it was still very strange. Noel, who was one of my greatest supporters, stayed with the JKS and with my increasing number of venues and the clubs in the UK, the JKS GB & Ireland (renamed after Seamus left), was on the up.

Within a year or so Cathal quit karate. Seamus followed shortly after. I never heard a word from or about either of them after Ian brought all his members under the JKS banner when Seamus quit training. I hope they are happy and I still feel they would have done well within our growing group, but it was a valuable lesson. People don't so much change as fail to show all their sides when you first meet them. I am convinced Seamus was influenced hugely by Cathal and Cathal's need to be the head honcho's right-hand man. Before I arrived he could easily cope with Ian, who was the only other good fighter in the group, but it was such a small pond in which to swim. When I arrived, I not only presented a threat in training, I also attracted interest from other dojos and groups. I had always been aware that within any dojo there is a certain proportion of students who just like to coast, who turn up to training, feel strong, effective and good, but never really go outside their comfort zone. This is fine, karate is for everyone. But this was the first time I had seen someone like that affect a whole group, the possible karate journey of many young, eager – and some seriously talented – karate-*ka*. Seamus and Cathal had good students who never fulfilled their potential because Cathal perhaps felt intimidated and Seamus was sold a line: sold the indisputable fact that I was English, therefore a liar, as such, I shouldn't be trusted.

*

Arrangements for the course developed rapidly. We had put an advert into *Shotokan Karate Magazine* and the interest had been widespread. Gayle's phone was hopping with calls from the UK. I was unsure if most of them knew they were calling Ireland, but many karate-*ka* were eager to talk to me about Yumoto Sensei and their excitement at his upcoming visit. The course was fully booked, with seventy-five black belts attending the three-day event. Ian, with a few of his students from his JKS-affiliated club, travelled over with the plan to take his second-degree black belt. The two JKS-affiliated clubs in the UK were also in attendance and together we represented about 20 per cent of those on the course. The remaining 80 per cent, as far as I was concerned, were potential members, and all we had to do was sell the JKS to them.

Yumoto Sensei did a wonderful job. He moved with such fluidity and taught with such humour that people were instantly smitten, like I knew they would be. I translated during the day and also at night, when Yumoto Sensei was surrounded by a crowd hungry for anecdotes and insights into whatever topic of conversation was of the moment. He talked freely about his time competing, his time on the Instructors' Course, about various technical points – and then the conversation turned to me. Someone had asked him about my time in Japan. He happily told them how hard I had trained on the Instructors' Course; how tough it had been for me. At one point he imitated how I must have cried myself to sleep each night, in a benevolently mocking manner. The audience lapped it up, although it felt odd to be talked about as if I wasn't there, whilst simultaneously translating the to-and-fro conversation like a tennis umpire with Tourette's.

The seminar finished with much praise from all. Many

serious-looking, beefy guys introduced themselves, asked about my plans for the JKS and made assurances that I would be hearing from them. With a meaningful handshake they were gone and I knew there were other possible converts on the horizon. I had also been talking all weekend to Uri, a talented fourth-degree black belt who had come over from Israel. He was interested in joining the JKS and affiliating his national group. He left with all the information he needed and was a member less than a month later. But the greatest triumph was Peter. He had helped facilitate the whole weekend, so I had taken care of him and his partner, Sally, throughout the various social gatherings. This wasn't done to endear myself to them, but was merely out of gratitude. Then at the end of the course Peter asked could we talk.

'So, I have been thinking about my future,' he started off. It was a promising opener.

'How can I help?' I knew exactly how I could help.

'Well, I'm not really interested in the JKS, but I *am* interested in working with you and Yumoto Sensei.' This was surprising: I was trying to sell the JKS, not Yumoto Sensei, let alone me. Although the JKS was only three years old, it had great legitimacy with Taguchi Sensei and the Instructors' Course. I thought it was a group with which he would be eager to affiliate.

'Whatever you want,' I said. We needed a greater presence in the UK and Peter could fit that role. He had a ready-made set-up with a squad and admin procedures, and as he was a full-time instructor, he had the time and inclination to put the effort into what it takes to run a group. In the brief gap of time we had, we set about formulating a plan. The finer brush strokes would be added later, but for now Peter wanted to be in the group for his guys. It added greater legitimacy to his membership and his keen young black belts would be exposed to the wider world of karate. I offered him the role of chairman. We needed a stronger direction in the UK and I thought Peter would be the perfect ambassador. Seamus had left six weeks before, so this would create balance within the UK- and Irish-based group, helping to implement the ideas of a third way. He accepted immediately and so the JKS GB & Ireland suddenly became a viable and sustainable group. Peter's initial comment of disinterest in the JKS *per se* still niggled, however. He wanted to work with Yumoto Sensei and me, so I believed I could convince him of the other benefits of JKS affiliation. Besides, in the space of six months, we had gone from nothing to twenty affiliated dojos across the UK and Ireland. Whatever happened, I knew our new chairman would be sold on the idea sooner or later.

The following week Peter called. 'What are you doing for Easter?' I had already booked flights to spend the holiday with Tor, and told him so, presuming he wasn't going to suggest we spend the weekend together, bromance style. 'That's a shame, as I'm teaching in Germany and it would be really good if you could come along.'

He went on to explain he had built up a friendship with an instructor in Germany. Guus had been a top competitor for the German National Team and was now a full-time instructor based in Heidelberg. Over the last few years they had started doing joint courses and one was scheduled for the Easter weekend. They were popular and it was decided a third instructor would be needed. I spoke to Tor. Graciously, understandingly, supportively, she told me I had to go. So new flights were booked and several weeks later I found myself at Frankfurt airport being collected by an athletic-looking, smiling German.

Guus showed me to his brand-new convertible VW Golf and soon we were zooming down the *autobahn*. He was cool and charismatic and seemed to be somewhat of a local celeb within the commune of Heidelberg. We made our way to his three-bedroom apartment (which I later found out he rented for the same monthly rate that was paid for a room in Dublin) and then we headed to his dojo. It was wonderful – the first full-time dojo I had been to in Europe. Apart from the competition mats on the floor, which I found difficult to adjust to, the venue was terrific. Trophies lined one side of the large training area and the reception was separated by a low-level wall, just the right height to allow eager parents to sit down and watch their young karate-*ka*. The reception was also fitted with a large counter, which, I was pleasantly reassured, doubled as a bar. But for now we were there to train. Peter and his students (he was bringing some of his top guys) wouldn't be arriving until later, so Guus had suggested on the car ride over that we could train this afternoon. He had dragged along two of his young students and they were already in the far corner, warming up.

I got changed and tiptoed onto the mats. The two teenagers nodded a welcome but took the introductions no further, so at a loss to know what to do – I think they spoke as much English as I spoke German – I wandered over to the *makiwara*, a well-used striking post in the corner. It had been a long time since the days when Takahashi Sempai had made Sueki and I do a thousand punches on each hand on the Headquarters' *makiwara*, so I thought I should give this one a go. I punched it as tentatively as a punch could be. It sprung back with a satisfying willow-ness. It felt good, so I hit it again, a little harder. Ah, I remember this feeling! I hit it again. And again. It was a great *makiwara* and had obviously been pounded in the dojo for some time. Okay, it was training time, let's go for it. I hit it again – CRACK! I looked down, trying to feel what I had broken of myself, when I noticed the clean sever of the striking post just at the base.

'What have you done?' Guus walked in just to see me break part of his dojo.

'Umm … sorry.' I didn't really know what to say. I'd only just met the guy and I was afraid I had scuppered any chance for an Anglo-German *entente cordiale*. He marched over as only a German can, and put out his hand.

'Congratulations! I've promised for years that anyone who could break that *makiwara* would get a year's free training. You are very welcome – although it will be a hell of a commute,' he concluded with a twinkle in his eye. Guus and I are going to get on, I thought.

Training started. Guus was obviously a sports karate-*ka*. He bounced, rather than moved, like Tigger who occasionally reverted to being a tiger, pouncing with an assured bellicosity. Despite my natural ambivalence to the sporting aspect of our art, I liked Guus. He moved well. The class was a long gauntlet of *kumite* drills and free sparring, but it was relaxed, a far cry from the intense *kumite* sessions of the Headquarters. I fought the nodding teenagers as well. One, Joseph, was tall and lanky for his age. He seemed twice my height and half my weight – at least he moved as if he were. Fists and feet came flying with unbelievable speed, but were exceptionally light to block. At times I struggled with his level, but as he lacked true power in his technique, I eventually came out on top. That was then, and he later went on to grow even more, put on some muscle and become All-Styles World Champion. I was glad I met him when he was young!

Peter arrived that evening and the three of us spent a

relaxing night at Guus's before the course started the following day. We arrived at the venue, a local sports centre, fresh and ready for action. However, a disappointing number of students were waiting for us. Peter's half-dozen senior grades made up most of the black belts and there was a scattering of colour belts that made the numbers up to twenty participants. The plan was to run two classes consecutively, divided by grade, but with such small numbers there was no point and we didn't need such a large space. Guus commanded everyone to follow him back to his dojo. Apparently the large sports hall was free to use for all local members of the sporting federation, so he just booked it on the off-chance we could fill it. As we hadn't, the course was moved back to his dojo. It felt better to be in a smaller space, but I couldn't help think that this course was all a bit haphazard. I was used to booking a venue and then feeling intense pressure to fill it. Guus never had such concerns and could use facilities for free – he certainly lacked one of my main motivators, and I didn't know if that was a good or a bad thing.

After the first day's training we retreated to a bar and ate and drank the local fare. It was nice to mix with Peter's students: mostly teenagers, they were fierce, tough, talented and loyal. They wore with pride the badges of Kaizenkan, the name of Peter's dojo. All were members of his squad that had travelled the world, achieving competition success at the highest level. Towards the end of the night Peter gave me a wink and called his crew over.

'Right guys, you know we have joined the JKS.' Nods of acknowledgment came from the half-dozen assembled acolytes. 'So I'm sorry to say that you are off the Kaizenkan team.'

Ranging from thirteen to nineteen years old, they managed

to hold in their anguish fairly well, showing even more toughness then they had in the dojo. They had a lot invested in Kaizenkan and Peter.

'But I'm happy to say you are now members of the JKS Great Britain team!' It was mean, but funny, and I couldn't help but laugh at the young lads. 'So you better up your game because now we will be going up against Japan!' Their distress was quickly converted to joy and then rapidly flipped to trepidation as the JKS opened up a whole new world of elite karate. Peter left them to ponder such changes and made his way to the toilet.

'I've just had a full conversation in German,' he explained on his return, beaming with pride.

'I didn't know you could speak German,' I replied, wondering about the type of conversation he would be having in the loo.

'I can't,' he said, hands on his hips. 'I was walking back from the toilet and I sneezed. Someone said "*gesundheit*", so I said "*danke*" and they said "*bitte*". How cool is that?'

'Yeah, great.' Peter was funny and I liked him a lot. He had a tough, aloof exterior in the dojo, but he was very quickly letting me see the other side of him. It would take many years before I could say he was one of my best friends, but we were off to a very good start.

The course was okay, we all taught well, ate well, drank even better and left having had a fun weekend. Guus and Peter were disappointed by the turn-out, as previous courses had attracted sixty or seventy participants and its popularity had been growing – I hoped I wasn't the reason for the dramatic and sudden decline in favour. They were gracious, though, and decided that after expenses, I would get the lion's share of profits. I was deeply grateful as I needed the money.

I didn't quite snatch the money from their hands, but didn't really resist their proposal for as long as I should have done. I felt a great alliance with these guys. I also felt indebted to them; they had given me their friendship and faith without question. It was a far cry from Seamus three months ago. Also, Guus wanted in. He was looking for direction in Germany and he felt the JKS was the way forward. He knew Peter and seemed to like me and wanted to be part of the group. My only surprise of the weekend was finding out that Peter was now 5th dan.

'Ah, what can you do?' he said when I questioned him about it. 'The BMAA awarded it to me a few weeks ago, as it's been five years since my last grading.' I should have said something, as he was now JKS, but couldn't. He had been so kind to me and was, in actual fact, my senior. Our respective grades now ratified that in some way. I let it pass.

I returned home and called Yumoto Sensei about Guus's desire to affiliate. It was a great conversation and I started to think I was actually making an impact in Europe. The JKS had been so small since we had lost the court case in 1999 and changed our name. When I moved to Ireland the only other JKS-affiliated group was Norway, but they were also affiliated to Richard Amos' WTKO and weren't particularly active within the JKS. Now we had the UK, Israel and Germany. Plus we decided to plan for a JKS summer camp. Koyama Sempai was still based in France and although the group he worked for had left the JKS to affiliate to another group, he was still JKS and had a good group of loyal students. A few emails later, it was decided that we would run the first JKS European Summer Camp with Ireland, Britain, Germany and France. We would add to this by inviting each other to conduct annual technical seminars in each other's countries

– it would be a way to build bridges and develop a strong European base.

I was excited about the prospect of being invited to each of the countries and at the same time petrified that I had committed to having at least three national seminars in Ireland, as well as one more from a senior instructor from Japan. Dojo numbers were increasing back at home, but I still felt that intense pressure. Travelling abroad, or even to a dojo in Ireland, was fun. I could teach whatever I wanted, be a star for a day and then be fed, watered, paid and sent on my merry way: all the perks of life as a karate sensei without the responsibility. However, building up a sustainable group in Ireland went far beyond the small pressure of running a dojo. I was well into the realms of people management, handling expectations, massaging egos and bumbling my way through the nuances of Irish sensibilities, so perhaps my degree in anthropology hadn't been a complete waste of time.

I returned to Dublin after my Easter jaunt and started to push the idea of a summer camp in Germany to affiliated dojos in JKS GB & Ireland. I knew Peter would lead the charge in the UK, so I felt less pressure to convince the English folk, but we needed a few Irish to attend as well. I spoke to Ian in the hope that he could bring some of his guys, which he graciously agreed to do. I had thin pickings from my club: I really only had low grades and convincing someone who had been training only a matter of months to travel to Germany for a training camp was a tall order. Fortunately, I had Maz on my side. Since starting at the dojo back at my very first class, she had become a regular face. Six months before she had wanted to start a dance class and her boyfriend had wanted to try karate. He then had to relocate to the UK for work, so to 'show him' she had begun karate. She was smart, determined and stubborn, with a partner in the UK; no wonder we became best friends. It had become a tradition to go for drinks after training on Wednesdays at the Iveagh Gym in the centre of town. One pint flowed over to many more and it was during one of these midweek frenzies that I mentioned in passing the seminar in Germany. By the next class she had convinced another girl, Lisa, to come along. At least there would be three of us representing the Hombu Dojo.

The summer of 2003 was warmish but dull – something I would learn was a typical Irish summer. I longed to see the sun and as I felt I had worked so hard since arriving nine months ago, the prospect of a 'holiday' in Germany was very exciting. Maz, Lisa and I arrived early on the Wednesday and met Guus in the centre of Heidelberg for lunch and a pint. The sun beamed down and we set about enjoying the local beverages. Guus was a perfect host. Not a big drinker, he sat with us and soberly enjoyed the banter. After several hours he took a phone call: Koyama Sempai had arrived with his students at the dojo and was awaiting further instructions.

'His students are staying at the dojo, I'll have to go and let them in,' Guus informed us.

'I'm coming with you.' I downed my pint.

'But … we're drinking,' Maz protested. After all it was Wednesday and this was the day we normally drank.

'I have to go, my sempai is waiting.'

Maz pouted as only the French can. I wasn't sure she understood, but I had to greet my sempai. I hadn't seen him since he left Japan in the summer of my first year of the Instructors' Course. We jumped into Guus's convertible and motored over to the dojo. As we approached, Koyama Sempai stood at the entrance as his students peered through the window, looking at the trophies. I was a bit drunk, a bit nervous and a bit giddy at being away 'on holiday'. Before Guus had fully stopped I unbuckled my seatbelt, stood up and gave a deep bow followed by an '*Osu*, Sempai.' The fact that the car juddered with the handbrake added to my uneasiness and I lurched forward with the bow, nearly ending up sprawled over the windscreen, increasing the appearance of inebriation. Koyama Sempai was as gracious as always, ignoring my intoxication with all things German. I jumped out and we shook hands. He has really small hands, which produce an enormous amount of pressure – the stiletto heel of handshakes. He looked relaxed, happy and fit. He still had the huge body mass that he shifted about like a tectonic plate, inching slowly in whatever direction, ready to explode like a volcano at any moment. I was looking forward to training with him, and I was looking forward to teaching with him. This would be the first time I would be teaching alongside another Headquarters instructor – on the same ticket, so to speak.

The camp was fantastic. Guus, with his sporting karate background, taught competition fighting. I trained in his class and remember thinking that I wished I had been taught this as a kid, or at least before I had gone to Japan. I had never been shown tactics or even considered attacking off-line. Not even knowing there was a line, I usually attacked straight on, normally onto a fist.

Peter had a wealth of experience, having trained with Ishii Sensei since he was a child. He had also come through the ranks at the infamous Aberdeen Karate Club. Peter was tough, very tough. He taught great classes, but expected the best from people. I had chosen well for the position of chairman. He had presence, was publicly standoffish and was the opposite of me – I think we complimented each other well. Plus he was funny and I liked him. Koyama Sempai was awesome.

He moved with such fluidity, power and poise. The weight of Japan had been lifted from his shoulders and he was now free, lightly moving across the dojo floor, teaching in a relaxed, friendly manner. He was instantly adored by everyone in the dojo, and in the bar afterwards his loyal students beamed with pride that their sensei had been discovered. With around fifty participants, the event was a success in every possible way. Hungover, we made our way back to our respective countries on the Monday morning. By the end of the week Guus had booked the venue for the same time next year and his JKS membership had been approved by Japan.

Two months later Takahashi Sempai arrived in Dublin. This time Ishii Sensei had lost the political power to prevent us holding a seminar in the Republic. I felt sorry for Seamus and Cathal, who lacked the faith and had left what they thought was a sinking ship. It wasn't. The seminar was fully booked with participants from across Ireland as well as the UK, Germany, Norway and France. Takahashi Sempai was on fire. He zipped from one technique to the next. In his mid-thirties, this was the first in what would become a regular part of his life – travelling and teaching for JKS-affiliated organizations all over the world. He was in his element and with his basic English, he ingratiated himself with everyone in attendance. Until then, most European karate-*ka* would have only experienced the aloof karate sensei: instructors who taught and then left, never to be seen until the next annual training session or camp. Takahashi Sempai was different. Outside the dojo he was equally as accessible.

After training on the Saturday Maz had organized a trip to the Guinness Storehouse, and Takahashi Sempai came along with the pack of eager karate tourists. After the formalities of finding out how Guinness was made, we climbed to the top of the famous facility at St James' Gate and had several pints in the 360° bar, taking in the view of the whole of Dublin. After a quick return to hotels we made our way back into the city centre and enjoyed food and drink in true Dublin style. Takahashi Sempai was there throughout, chatting with students, answering questions, telling stories and laughing at jokes that I am sure he didn't quite understand. Occasionally he would call me over to translate for someone, although I tried to keep this to a minimum as I had my own networking to do. It was great to be in his company, but the stress of the Instructors' Course was a recent memory. I was twitchy around him and wanted to enjoy the fruits of my hard work. I hoped I wasn't being negligent and was constantly glancing over to check if he was okay. Old habits die hard, even though I was several thousand miles away from Japan and several pints past *compos mentis*.

Sunday's training was tough. Not because we were all hungover, but because Takahashi Sempai was hungover. I had seen that look during the dark days in Japan: he was ready to purge himself of last night's abuse and we were there for the ride. I vaguely remember being paired up with Peter doing endless repetitions of *kumite* drills. I felt so alive, fuelled on by endorphins and pride. Peter, for his part, was popping out techniques with grit and determination. At one point during a lull in proceedings I sidled over to him and said that this training was harder than the Instructors' Course. 'Really?' came the reply. I think that's all he needed and suddenly he found a new reserve of energy. Damn, I thought, now I have to up my game too. By the end of the session my belt was dripping with sweat, something that hardly ever happened even in Japan.

✲

Several of the French and Germans weren't returning home until Monday morning, so I mentioned to Maz that we should have organized something for them. Leave it with me, came the response. By the end of training Maz had secured the function room above the Oliver St John Gogarty, one of the most famous pubs in one of the most famous parts of Dublin. About twenty participants remained and had enough energy to make their way to that Mecca of binge-drinking: cobblestoned Temple Bar. Up the winding stairs, we entered into a leprechaun-leaping, whiskey-swilling, green-wearing stage set of a room and soon settled into the Irishness of it all. Food, which wasn't particularly good, was eaten with joy, and beer, which was great, was drunk with enormous enthusiasm. At one point during the madness a young lad from France challenged Takahashi Sempai to a break-dancing competition. France won, but Japan retorted with an air-chair competition whereby both athletes had to hold the pain-inducing pose until someone gave in or collapsed, which the French challenger did after some considerable time. Takahashi Sempai celebrated his victory by buying everyone in our party a drink. It was a wonderful night and so far away from the constraints and conformity of our lives in Japan. This was happy karate.

The following day, after escorting Takahashi Sempai to the airport and making sure all was in order, I slouched back outside to wait for the bus and make the winding journey back to Dublin 6. I realized I had been in Dublin for a year. What a year! My clubs had had another large influx in September, we had just run our first successful JKS Ireland seminar, free from interference from Ishii Sensei, and I started to have a little money in my pocket. I stood up, walked across the road to the taxi rank, got into the first waiting car and asked the driver to take me to Rathmines. I had no idea how much this would cost, but I deserved it. To Rathmines, driver – I'm a professional karate instructor!

Half an hour later we approached Gayle's house. Do I say 'drop me off here' or 'pull over here' I mused. I'd never taken a taxi in English before.

'Pull me off here, please,' I said. I may have been a professional karate instructor, but I was still a clown.

FIVE

When I was eighteen Ishii Sensei had taken me to Japan. Charging a fortune, he had acted like a native tracker, guiding me through the dense flora and fauna of the faraway East. It had been an invaluable experience and I wanted to replicate it for the JKS GB & Ireland members. Still flush from the success of Takahashi Sempai's seminar, I sent an email around to club instructors asking if anyone was interested. The reply was a resounding yes.

I wanted to replicate what Ishii Sensei had offered: firstly because he no longer offered it and secondly because it was a great idea, although I would do it for cheaper. Ten years earlier I had paid well over two grand for an all-inclusive two-week trip. I had done the maths, I could do it for £1,350. So I put a package together and sent it out. Twelve eager seniors made the quick decision to come along. On 24 January 2004 we boarded a plane to Tokyo to attend *Kangeiko*[1] at the Headquarters. Peter and Guus had decided to come, as well as several of their top students. Ian had also come along with Jack, his senior brown-belt student. For Jack it was the first time on a plane, train and boat. With Tor by my side we had a good, manageable and keen crew and I really looked forward to showing them what Japan had to offer.

1. *Kangeiko* – Cold Training. A traditional Japanese way of re-dedicating yourself to training for the forthcoming year.

The idea was to stay in Tokyo for a week and complete the *Kangeiko* at the Headquarters, training every morning at 7 a.m. It was quintessentially Japanese. We would then train in the evenings with my sensei and sempai, leaving enough time during the day to visit the madness of Tokyo. After this I had arranged, with the help of Sueki, to train at his newly opened dojo and then to travel north into the mountains, to train with Yokose Sensei. A 7th dan with the JKS, he was a sempai of Yumoto Sensei and I had trained with him several times whilst at the Headquarters. He had a large dojo two hours outside the metropolis and had readily accepted Sueki's suggestion and even insisted we do a homestay with his many students. The final part of the trip would be some well-deserved R & R in Hakone, enjoying the hot springs and greenness in the foothills of Mount Fuji.

After months of organization we found ourselves at Narita Airport, drinking Starbucks, waiting for the Narita Express to take us to Ikebukuro. I felt at home, as if I had never been away. My little line of ducks followed me as I navigated the chaos of the urban crush. I couldn't believe how much I had missed my home, my Japan. My consciousness flipped – orientating to the Orient! Japanese gushed effortlessly when I spoke and it was as if the turmoil of my mind over the last eighteen months was due to the suppression of my Eastern being. It was strange, but I felt good. We checked in, I assigned rooms, allowed showers to be taken and then insisted we meet, ready for lunch, in thirty minutes – we had all travelled through the night, but this was no time to sleep. An hour later, my merry band scrambled behind me as I gave them a whirlwind tour of Shinjuku. I quickly found that if I waited for people, progress was delayed, so I abandoned compassion and just marched on. Their fear of being lost focused their minds and whenever I did happen to glance behind, they were elbowing innocent bystanders out the way to keep up, like any Pro-Granny Scrum Maestro you could find on the subway fifty metres below.

As I had predicted, and as it started to get dark, the spirits of my group started to wane. We were in Shinjuku: I knew the *izakayas*[2] opened at 5 p.m., so I looked up to spot the nearest big-nosed, red-faced sign of Tengu. Sure enough, several were within sight, so I made my way to the nearest. I bustled the guys in and they placed their shoes neatly to one side and slid into the dug-out beneath the low table. There was a certain anticipation in the air, and all being Japan virgins, I think they expected nothing but sushi. The waiter came, panic-stricken at being confronted by a sea of white faces. I put his mind at rest, ordered *nomihou-dai* (the infamous Japanese all-you-can-drink menu) for everyone and set about ordering threes of certain foods. The beers arrived and they sipped, then drank, then gulped. More drinks were ordered, and by the end of the second pint, Peter piped up.

'How much are these?' The price that they had all paid had included everything except alcohol. They had nothing to pay except the drinks bill at the end of each evening, so I guess that was niggling somewhere in between gulps of his Kirin Ichiban.

'Well, I've ordered *nomihou-dai* for everyone.' I was met with quizzical looks. 'So we can drink whatever is on this menu.' I held the page of Japanese squiggles in my hand. 'As much as we want … for two hours.'

'How much is that?' Peter had a certain Scottish panic about his voice.

---

2. *Izakaya* – A Japanese bar, half tapas restaurant, half Ozzie-style watering hole.

'1800 yen each.' The same quizzical looks. 'About £12.'

'What?' A wave of incredulity swept the table. 'So what exactly is on that list?' and they were off. By the time the food started to arrive, they had already discovered the delights of sours in all its fruity formats. Wine was drunk, then whiskey, but it wasn't until they made their way to *sake* that their night became a blur. Like any *izakaya*, food arrived on small plates and at one point I had to stop everyone from piranha-ing every morsel as soon as it hit the table.

'Guys!' I stood, trying to be commanding, 'Food will keep on coming. We are here all night and we can order as much as we want. This is Japan – small dishes will continuously arrive and you can nibble away!'

'Ah, so it's only the beer we have to gulp down?' Peter piped up and the group cheered. Only Guus complained that he had to pay the *nomihou-dai* fee, but had only drunk three Cokes (until I pointed out that each Coke was 700 yen, therefore I had *saved* him money). We made our way back to the *Ryokan*[3] and fell onto our futons.

The next day I woke to find my mental balance, my perfect equilibrium of East and West, had been shattered. I was back in the torture of two years ago. My emotions shut down and Tor looked at me as if I were a stranger. We made our way to the Headquarters and I clearly remember holding on to the door, taking a deep breath and then forcing myself to open it and walk through to face my demons, to face my cell, to face the life I thought I had escaped. Sueki was there, his face lighting up as soon as he saw me. He rushed

3. *Ryokan* – Small, Japanese inn, full of rice paper screens and creaky floor boards ready to repel ninja attacks

over and we shook hands, a far more reserved greeting than the last time I had seen him.

'So, is that her?' He peered over my shoulder, looking at Tor. He was obviously interested in meeting my girlfriend. I nodded and he bustled past, introducing himself in bad, clumsy, but adorable English. Tor responded with an '*Osu*, Sensei' with the other guys instantly following suit. Sueki glanced round, acknowledged the group and then returned to me. There was no time to talk, so with a hand on his shoulder I said we'd catch up later.

We made our way into the dojo. I directed everyone to the changing rooms and then knocked on the instructors' room door and entered. Yumoto Sensei and Takahashi Sempai sat, drinking tea.

'*Osssssssu*, Sucotto!' Yumoto Sensei beamed and Takahashi Sempai smiled warmly too. It was lovely to be back and the nerves melted away. I sat for a while and chatted about the group I had brought. Then, excusing myself, I got changed and entered the dojo. My old friends were there to greet me. Familiar faces, that had last seen me struggle through the worst period in my life, now looked at me afresh. Various '*Hisashiburi* sensei' (it's been a while) and 'Sensei, *genki sou*' (you look well), were followed by handshakes. A few students I was closer to commented on how pretty Tor was, but before I knew it I just had enough time to give my formal greeting, '*Yoroshiku Onegaishimasu*', to Shima Sempai and Yamada Sempai before the class started.

An hour later, sweat dripping from noses, my group made their way to the changing room, relieved but, I could tell, invigorated. Takahashi Sempai sidled up beside me.

'So are you doing instructors' training?'

My nerves instantly kicked in. Think fast, Scott.

'I have to take my guys for breakfast.' I gave him a cheeky smile and he took it well. 'Maybe tomorrow,' I said, although this would become a running joke, with him asking me every morning if I would train with them and me explaining the incompetence of my guys in everything from ordering breakfast to buying train tickets to crossing the roads – I feared I would lose one or two if I left them to their own devices for an hour. Of course, I didn't. I also didn't fear the instructors' training – it definitely wasn't fear. Instructors' training was always easier during *Kangeiko* and I knew I was well beyond the days of being beaten up, but still I couldn't bring myself to train. I later tried to analyse my reaction, as I had expected that I would train and had mentioned it to Tor and Peter. I think it was the control.

Since the summer of 2002 I had regained my independence. I couldn't afford to lose that again. At the time it was a simple knee-jerk reaction. I hadn't expected Takahashi Sempai to ask me to join the instructors' class every day I was in the dojo, which would continue like an orchestrated dance every time I returned to Japan for the next decade. I also didn't expect myself to reject every request. In fact, that one moment was the first time I had said no to him: not that I knew it at the time, but this was the start of the end. So early on I had broken that bond between sempai and *kohai*[4]. Years later Sueki would comment on how clever I was. I had never called Takahashi Sempai 'Sempai'. I always called him sensei when talking to him, although he was my sempai in every way. Sueki thought I was clever to maintain that distance throughout the Instructors' Course and beyond – the inference was he wished he could do the same. But for now I just said it. Something instinctive mad me leap out of the way and I jokingly made

4. *Kohai* – One's Junior.

haste and escaped out the door to have breakfast. However, I would see this little moment concluded in a big way many years later.

The week in Tokyo went well. The guys trained hard and I interspersed sessions with trips to mountains, temples, shops, rush hour trains, crazy dinners, red-light districts, parochial dojos and the climbing of more stairs than they had ever seen in their lives. On the final day everyone was given a certificate of completion from Yumoto Sensei. Bottles of beer and various nibbles had been arranged around the dojo and the guys got ready to celebrate their success with an 8 a.m. drink.

'Sucotto, make the toast!' Yumoto Sensei asked me to kick off proceedings. I did as requested and with a booming '*Osu*' from Yumoto Sensei, drinks were downed, food was nibbled and the party went into hyper-drive for the rest of the day. Several hours in I remember looking around the Headquarters. Groups of karate-*ka* had gathered around my guys. Chatting, exchanging email addresses, numbers, inside leg measurements. For them, it was equally as novel as it was for my members. I sat talking to Takahashi Sempai, Sueki and Hirota, our *kohai* who was just about to graduate the course. We discussed developments in Europe as all around my guys ingratiated themselves with their Eastern counterparts. Of course this was done by drinking games and at one point I noticed Nirei-San, a fifth degree black belt with the Headquarters, had unfortunately been caught by Peter in a round of challenging *kampais*. Nirei-San, as tough as he was, was a mild-mannered salaryman[5] in his normal life and not used to the hard drinking of the canny Scot. Before long, I saw it get the better of him as he explained he had to go to the toilet in quite good English – I didn't even know

5. *Salaryman* – A Japanese office worker.

he spoke a word of it. I watched as he left Peter's table and made his way to the toilet. As he passed the *makiwara* he stopped. No, don't do it, I thought – but he couldn't resist. He squared up to the punching post, positioned himself for a strong *gyaku zuki*[6], the go-to technique of any karate-*ka*, and fired. Missing completely, he lurched forward, forcefully connecting the post with his head. It sprung back pushing him to the ground, where he lay, flat out.

'Hirota, is Nirei-San okay?' No one had seen, so I let Hirota take care of him, hoping my lot didn't kill any of the others through alcohol and misuse of dojo equipment. They didn't and a great dojo party eventually concluded. Of course we changed venues several times, going to the *nijikai* and *sanjikai*, the second and third parties, losing more and more drunk salarymen as we went. Finally we crawled into bed after catching the last train home sometime after midnight.

I remember lying on my futon, Tor by my side, on that final evening in Tokyo. I had been in fear for most of the trip. Fear of being beaten – there was no other type of fear. And yet I knew they wouldn't lay a finger on me. It was strange, like the ghost of my old psychosis had come back to haunt me and I was feeling the pain of a long-amputated limb. On the flip side, I had been treated with such respect. Peter, Guus and the rest of the crew had been blown away by the hospitality, and I had been blown away by their respect. I was unquestioningly part of the instructors' group. I had been away for eighteen months and feared I would be dropped. If anything, I was more included than when I had been training here daily. I lined up with my sempai, trained with them during *Kangeiko*, ate, drank and laughed with them. I felt part of them. When I lived here, I was different from them.

6. *Gyaku zuki* – reverse punch.

Now that I didn't live here I was different from the other *gaijin* I had brought. One of our group would later say that people normally go tick-tock tick-tock, but as soon as Scott arrives in Japan he goes tock-tick tock-tick. I understood what he was trying to say.

The following day we made our way to Sueki's private dojo. Hirota taught first. He was terrific and had become everything I thought he would. I taught second and then Sueki finished with a flourish of great *kumite* drills. We stayed the night at a crazy, super *sento* – a Japanese bathhouse – drinking and arm-wrestling strangers well into the night. The following day we made our way to Yokose Sensei's dojo, north of Tokyo. I understood that he had a small private dojo, but my directions lead to a large sports centre. I entered and asked about possible karate training.

'Ah, yes. Are you Scott Sensei? Yokose Sensei is expecting you.' The lady gave me further directions. We found the changing rooms, changed and made our way into a large multi-purpose sports hall. There must have been well over a hundred black belts in perfectly formed lines neatly punctuating the dojo. Yokose Sensei stood off to one side as another gentleman conducted a warm up. I instructed my guys to make a separate line at the back, behind the one line of white belts, and went over to greet Yokose Sensei.

'Ah, Sucotto,' came the familiar greeting. We chatted for a little and then I excused myself to take part in the warm-ups. As I made my way to the back of the dojo, Mark, my French-Moroccan *kohai* walked towards me. He had done well in the eighteen months since I had last seen him. He had started to assist Yokose Sensei with his massive classes and was doing everything in his power to enter the Instructors' Course. As I approached, he held a focus pad and gestured for me to hit it – whenever two karate-*ka* meet, it is compulsory for violence to be involved. Holding it in front of his stomach I went to make a front kick, but just before impact I changed and snapped my foot up and round to tap him lightly on the face with a roundhouse kick – I was showing off.

'That's why I want to do the Instructors' Course,' he said. 'So I can kick like that!'

I enquired how he was getting on, knowing that I could kick like that well before I entered the course. I have spoken to people who have known graduates of the course before and after. Unanimously, they all say the instructor in question never really changed their karate through the course, they just became 'more them'. It seems an odd concept, but Peter was once asked the same question and said the same thing. Mark had made great progress in the few years he had been in Japan, but I doubted the course would be the answer to all his dreams – nightmares, maybe. I wished him well and slotted into the line-up who were halfway through their warm-ups.

Training started, which like most training, was basic, with very little instruction. We started with *gyaku zuki* and Yokose Sensei idled past, informing me we were going to do a thousand punches. I passed on the good news to Peter, as we both immediately eased up. The count seemed to be self-replicating – as one black belt in the line-up finished counting ten, the next along eagerly took their turn to blast out the rhythm. Members of the trip, over various food and drink through the week, had mentioned how amazed they were by the great level of karate here, but were at a loss to understand how people became good.

Instruction, whether at the Headquarters or the three other dojos we visited, had ranged from very little to non-existent, but everyone was good. I now hoped they understood why – repetition. In the West we often learn from the top down. Things are explained, conceptualized and delivered in a way someone can think about, hopefully leading to a physical understanding. In the East it is from the bottom up. There is no need to explain, just do and copy. Hundreds lead to thousands of repetitions and eventually your body finds a way, occasionally leading to a mental understanding. This is how they learn *Kanji*, this is how they learn English, this is how they learn karate – and it works (for karate, not so much for English!).

Surrounded by a hundred junior black belts, all whipping out snappy punches with lovely form, poise and power, we were then rudely interrupted by a loud *thud*. I looked at Peter. 'What was that?' I mouthed. He shrugged. *Thud*. There is was again. *Thud*. And again. We looked around. It started to match the count of the fierce eight-year-old who was dictating our movements three metres to my left. *Thud … thud … thud*. I looked around for Yokose Sensei and soon found the source of our disturbance. Yokose Sensei had found a steel girder, one of the exposed supports of the centre. He must have decided he needed some *makiwara* practice and started pounding the innocent lump of metal and at the same time immediately became a legend within the membership of the JKS GB & Ireland. It was the talk of the evening and most evenings after that.

He was truly a tough man, but more importantly a gentle, genuine sensei who spent the next two days facilitating the most wonderful cultural exchange for my group. It was an experience money couldn't buy, with families opening up their homes to us. We had parties and adventures, fishing and hiking in the mountains during the day, followed by further parties with our host families in the evening. I had asked everyone to bring presents for their families, which they gave out on the first evening, but by the end of the two days everyone had received much more in return: bottles of *sake*, pots of various pickles, old pictures and paintings. Things that may just have been hanging around the families' homes, but were treasures as far as these innocent *gaijin* were concerned. We boarded the train two days later, with each family standing at the ticket gates, bowing deeply. Yokose Sensei waved, grinning broadly. I had not known him well when living in Japan, and I am sorry I hadn't. He was a wonderful gentleman and helped show my group the best part of what Japan could be.

Tor and I enjoying the hospitality of Yokose Sensei, Akiruno-shi, Japan, January 2004.

We had two days left in Japan and spent it in Hakone, relaxing in hot springs, drinking grapefruit sours and appreciating the natural beauty of the area. On the last night we sat around low-lying tables in a large twelve-*tatami*-matted room the *ryokan* had kindly allowed us to use for our nightly 'meetings'.

'So, best and worst.' Peter had called people to attention and was about to extract information from them. They looked puzzled. 'What was the best and worst part of the trip?' Alcohol helped fuel honesty and within minutes it was decided that we would go around the table and all have a turn. As we went from one person to the next, their input got longer and before we knew it, it had taken several hours to complete the cycle. I knew people had had a great time, what I didn't expect was that almost all of them launched into the worst part of the trip first. I hadn't noticed, being in my own mental turmoil, but during *Kangeiko* most had struggled. Maybe it was a combination of being away from family, being in such a foreign environment and sharing rooms with relative strangers. This combined with jet lag had led to a couple of difficult days midweek. However, they had supported each other, allowed themselves to be swept along and eventually got through to the other side, all the better for it. I was happy, and there were many 'best trip of my life'-type reviews. 'A trip money can't buy' was another common theme. They couldn't believe the simplicity of training, mostly *mae geri oi zuki*.[7]

'In fact, the best lesson was the class Scott taught,' Peter commented graciously.

Guus began by saying how he had been involved with Japanese instructors for the last thirty years. He had never experienced such friendliness, openness and humour from all the visiting instructors in Germany. 'I just can't fathom why they are so nice to us,' he concluded.

7. *Mae geri oi zuki* – the bog-standard front kick, stepping punch.

'Really?' Peter couldn't resist.

'No! Japanese instructors normally aren't this nice. Why are they so nice to us?'

Peter looked around. There were a few people rolling their eyes – two weeks of close proximity had created a final frosting of Anglo-German relations.

'BECAUSE OF SCOTT!' he bawled, probably louder than he had wanted to. There had been very few arguments during the trip. No fallings-out, just mild irritation on occasion. This was pressure being released, induced by Guus' blindness as to why the group had just had the 'best trip of their lives'. Thankfully Peter and Guus were good friends and amicable relations resumed immediately.

'Oh … okay.' Guus looked at me. 'Scott, *kampai.*' Everyone instantly joined in and there was one last resounding *kampai* to finish the night. The following day we made our way back to Narita and home. Okay, I thought. What next?

The trip really helped to cement the JKS GB & Ireland in the karate scene in the British Isles. Before the days of Facebook and Twitter, I am still amazed that we had such an impact so quickly. Since returning to Europe I had been frantically writing articles for *Shotokan Karate Magazine*. I had known the editor since the early days with Ishii Sensei and knew interesting articles would be well received. As I was writing *Karate Stupid* I was already into that mind set. Plus, living with Gayle, I seemed to be surrounded by the clicking of keyboards, and a critical eye was never too far from anything I committed to floppy disk – yes it was that long ago. So within a year I produced about ten articles for the magazine. With four issues per year, it meant I had a steady stream of free advertising.

At first these articles were mainly technical, addressing

topics I could easily see hadn't been talked about in the West, but which were common practice in the East. I am sure I wasn't reinventing the wheel, I was just lucky to be saying something that hadn't been talked about in a while and saying it as a newly graduated instructor just arrived on the scene, representing a new organization. Timing is everything. Of course, I was also interested in teaching more weekends. Apart from being lucrative – which as soon as I could subsist on my dojo, was not a motivating factor – I enjoyed teaching higher-level concepts to eager groups. During the week I would play about and experiment with ideas and ways to deliver my thoughts. Then at weekends I would present my findings in front of a new crowd, hoping to please – desperate to please. In fact I was deeply insecure about what I was doing. I was a thirty-year-old 4th dan. I wasn't senior in any way, so I went out of my way to make sure I did a good job. During our second year when the JKS GB & Ireland had started to grow, Peter said to me, 'I just expect someone to tap me on the shoulder and say "okay, time's up – get off now!"' I knew exactly what he meant. Why me? What do I have to offer? To this day I look in the mirror at my dojo and think 'well, that's a pile of crap!'

However, of almost equal proportion to my insecurity is my confidence. Whenever I walked into a dojo for the first time I reminded myself I had completed the Instructors' Course. It was just enough. I was slightly insecure, always projecting forward to what I could do, to what I had to do. The source of this insecurity was a mystery that I am sure a psychologist could make a good case-study of one day. However, I harnessed it, never allowing myself to stand still. When it got too much I looked back at what I had achieved and allowed myself to relax. So, with this in mind, I set about building a portfolio of dojos that liked what I did and would invite me to teach seminars at weekends. Dojos in the UK were the first to bite.

'Scott, we'd like to invite you to teach, but how much will it cost? Oh, £100, that's cheap – ah, but you live in Ireland, how much would it cost to fly you over?' At that point I would jump on the internet. Thank God for Ryanair. I would come back with a price. 'So I can get you over to teach for a day for less than £150? Are you free the start of May?'

It was an easy decision for people. I was cheap, accessible and with regular flights from Dublin I felt like I should be made an ambassador by Michael O'Leary. I was happy to stay in people's spare bedrooms rather than hotels, and more often than not I would fly into Bristol, stay with Tor and then we would travel to some new dojo on the appointed day. I'd teach and then we'd stay or make our way back to Bristol. I saw Tor, taught interesting classes to interested people and had my weekend paid for. I worked hard, though. I made notes of what I had taught and how I had taught it. I never wanted to repeat myself as I found very quickly that whenever I taught in the UK certain members from JKS-affiliated clubs would always attend, no matter where I was. I felt a huge responsibility to give them value for money. I couldn't short-change them and teach the same class I had done several weeks earlier elsewhere – even if just one stalker showed up.

I also made sure I never left the host out of pocket. I became astute at calculating how much money was in the room. A quick tally of adults and children in attendance, times the course fee, and I'd figured out how much profit was there. I knew what the host had to pay me, so I could see if the course was sustainable or not. Only on one occasion could I see that the course would run at a loss, so I offered to reduce my fee. They kindly refused, and I was paid and invited back.

That was behind everything I did. I wanted to be invited back. This was my job. They were the bosses. Everything I did had to be sustainable. So that meant a lot of cheap early morning Ryanair flights, followed by a lot of staying in spare rooms and making sure I didn't choose a meal that was vastly more expensive than my host's at the post-training pub party. Everything I did was considered and thought out. Maybe my OCD had returned, albeit in a more socially acceptable way. Whatever I was doing, it was working: I was building a solid number of dojos that liked what I did.

It wasn't always positive though. On one occasion, I found myself in Bristol with Tor, but no dojo to go to. Tor had suggested that I bring my *dogi* and we would go to train at her local club in Bath. She had been a member there on and off since university days and I fancied an opportunity just to train. We arrived at a bog-standard karate club. The local community centre hall had been hired and in traipsed an assortment of coloured belts and a few black belts. The instructor was a guy in his fifties, slightly overweight, but slimmer, I am sure, than most of his peers. Tor asked if we could train, he agreed, we paid and off we went.

It was odd to be training in a dojo in the UK after all these years. When I was a kid I would always take my *dogi* with me when on holiday with my parents. The local karate club would be found and off I would go. I was exposed to some good and some not-so-good clubs and got a real sense of what was out there. However, it had been years since I had found myself in such a situation. We started with basics, marching up and down the dojo as the instructor belched out commands, neither demonstrating nor instructing to any great degree. He kept on glancing in my direction, so I knuckled down and tried harder. Before long, the furtive glances gave way to blatant gawping, which gave way to him coming over and standing in front of me as I trudged *ad nauseam* up and down the hall. He didn't have the look of someone who was impressed and decided to instruct a little.

'No, look.' He gathered people round. 'When you make front stance you must lock out your back leg. Don't bend it, that's weak!' He concluded as if it were the most obvious concept in the world. His instruction then became entirely focused – on me. 'You must make stronger techniques.' Was he actually going to tell me to do it faster, harder, stronger? It was a cliché in the karate world that some senseis' instruction only amounted to superlatives, barking orders without any clear direction as to how to achieve such commands. He thought I was too relaxed, that I should tense up and make strong punches. I defiantly continued with my own karate. Eventually he gave up, but not before stopping the class. 'There is so much wrong with your karate, I don't know where to begin,' he concluded and walked off. I grinned and continued to train.

Several weeks later I taught a seminar with Peter in Leicester. I had decided I was going to 'teach' tube training over the weekend, and although it seems common practice now, at the time these drills were virtually unknown. I had asked Peter to collect as many used bicycle inner tubes as possible. He did, and we spent a busy Friday night cutting up and tying rubber tubes.

The next day I taught a mixture of familiar and unfamiliar faces. Peter's young lions roared as they got to grips with the tubes. They bounced from combination to combination as only youth can. Others didn't fare so well. There was one chap who became greener and greener throughout the hour-long session.

Ten minutes before the end I heard, 'Excuse me Sensei' and I turned round to see him dart for the toilet door, followed by sounds of vomiting. Oh dear, I thought. Too much? Before I knew it he was back, tube in hand, ready for the next set. I like you, I thought and soon we were both sitting in the community centre bar, enjoying a well-deserved pint.

Simon was a stand-up comic. He was also very funny. We chatted and drank, enjoying the start of what would become a long friendship.

At one point Tor stopped, mid-drink, 'Wait, do you do a joke about going round to friends' houses just before bedtime and filling their kids with chocolate and Red Bull, swinging them around the room and then leaving them for their parents to put to bed?'

'Well not for a while, but yeah, that's me.'

'Jiggidy, jiggidy, jiggidy!' Tor burst into a fit of laughter as I looked on, utterly confused.

Apparently Simon was more than a comic; he was a Perrier-nominated comic whom Tor had seen on TV years ago. He was also good at karate. He had spent a year training at the JKA headquarters in Ebisu, Tokyo, during its heyday. He had then returned to London and spent well over a decade training exclusively with Enoeda Sensei at Marshall Street. I was impressed.

At the time he was a wandering Ronin, a samurai without a master. With no dojo affiliation, he was free to train wherever he wanted. As he was doing comedy gigs the length and breadth of the country almost daily, schedules were checked, logistics put in place and before I knew it Simon was a regular fixture at the seminars the JKS were conducting. Before the year was out he became a member of Peter's dojo and a new senior figure within the group. During post-training drinks it quickly became apparent that Simon's business had close parallels to mine. He made a good, professional living based on providing a quality service to a couple of dozen comedy clubs. They booked him, he turned up on time, did a great job and left their customers happy. The club then booked him again. It was that simple. Of course, he was talented. Tor and I sat in his audience as often as we could and watched him transform into Simon the Performer. However, like any art, the business side of the show was equally important and I stole as many ideas from him as possible.

Invites were coming in from the UK with pleasant regularity but I had nothing from Ireland. It was strange – as if I were a pariah to be avoided. Then in late September 2003 I finally got my first connection outside the JKS. Paddy Casanova (I really haven't made the name up) invited me to teach in Dingle, a small village at the end of a peninsula located at the westerly edge of Ireland. I accepted and he sent me a train ticket the following month and off I set. It was impossible to get a train to Dingle, so the ticket took me as far as Tralee where he would be waiting to drive me the rest of the way.

I arrived to an empty but sunny train station. It was deserted. I strolled about for a while, then sat out front, looked at my watch and sat for a while longer. Eventually a tall, slender, bald gentleman arrived, looking flustered, and walked into the train station. Moments later he returned, glanced at me and then scurried back. I decided that had to be him and was just about to give chase when a deep English accent punctuated the silence.

'Are you Scott Langley?' Flustered man had returned again with a voice that didn't quite match, both in tone and accent. Paddy was English?

'Yes.' I stood up and shook his hand.

'I thought you'd be bigger,' he commented. I was sorry to disappoint, but unsure why. 'You know, from your pictures in *SKM*.' As if that were enough to explain my puzzled, embarrassed look.

I was escorted to an unloved Fiat Panda and off we set for the hour-long journey through winding country roads. Since then I have experienced this type of situation many times: thrust into a confined space with a complete stranger for a period of time, forced to make small talk until the journey's end. Fortunately I very quickly realized that Paddy was a wonderful, eccentric and interesting fellow, the type of person I often stumble across. But before our small talk was allowed to meander into a full-blown conversation Paddy noticed a hitchhiker on the side of the road. 'Ah, sure, why not,' he mumbled to himself.

So now I was in a Fiat Panda with two complete strangers. Was this a set up? Did Tor or Gayle know where I was? Did anyone know where I was? I hadn't even bought the train ticket so there was no paper trail.

My fears were interrupted by my phone. '*Mushi mushi. Hirota desu kado*!' It was Hirota, calling from the Headquarters.

'Ah, *mushi mushhh. Genki*?' A conversation ensued about a topic that has been lost in time. I hung up to find both Paddy and Mr Stranger had been listening intently.

'Was that Chinese?' Mr Stranger asked in a thick Kerry accent.

'No, Japanese … I lived there for a while,' I said, by way of explanation. 'In Tokyo.'

'Really? I know someone in Tokyo. Charlie. He's a tall guy, blond hair.' No, please don't ask, I thought. He couldn't possibly be going to ask. 'Yeah, he's been there for a while, teaches English, I think.'

'Er …' I gave the impression I was giving it a moment's thought. 'No, sorry, I don't.'

'Tall guy. Quite stocky? Plays rugby?' Paddy had joined in, but I thought he was taking the piss.

'Yeah, that's him,' Mr Stranger eagerly replied.

'He used to live in Hong Kong!' Paddy continued. The stranger nodded eagerly. 'Yeah, I know him. I was there about ten years ago. A great guy – what's he up to nowadays?' And they were off. The rest of the journey was consumed by their mutual friend and I thought, only in Ireland. It was small, parochial almost, but it was also cosy and reassuring. A comfort blanket of a country that wrapped itself around you in a nurturing, maternal way.

A short time later I heard a story about how a distraught wife had burst into her local Dublin garda station. Her husband had only fecked off down to Cork and had taken her house keys. She was locked out and had no idea what to do.

'What's the fecking idiot driving, missus?' the duty office enquired. He then got onto the radio and called patrol cars on the Cork Road. Within the hour the poor guy had been pulled over and told that his wife was locked out and he had to get his arse back to Dublin ASAP. Only in Ireland. I don't know if that story is true, but I think it is. And if it isn't, it could easily be. I was learning to love Ireland and all its quirks. With the invite from Paddy, and the super weekend that followed, I started to get more invites in the Republic.

In March 2004 Yumoto Sensei finally arrived on the shores of the Emerald Isle. One year after his planned visit, the tectonic plates of the JKS and TBKA political world had shifted. The success of the group and the growth in Europe had turned Taguchi Sensei's focus and Yumoto Sensei was allowed to visit. The seminar was a huge success. Most groups within Ireland were represented, and I set about ingratiating myself with these many strangers. One club joined on the spot. To be fair, they had been to the course I had taught for Paddy in Dingle six months earlier, so Yumoto Sensei was the icing on the cake. Kay and Humphrey Doody were familiar faces within the Irish karate scene and I am sure their support very early on began to ignite possibilities in the minds of the various onlookers.

Moving quickly on from that success, Peter and I set about organizing the JKS European Camp, which was to be held in London in October 2004. Whilst in Japan Taguchi Sensei had suggested that all the Headquarters instructors should pay a visit to the growing market of the UK and present a *tour de force* of JKS Karate. Peter and I couldn't believe our ears – it was only the previous year when he had tried to prevent Yumoto Sensei from teaching for us. Now, not only was he proposing a massive camp, but Taguchi Sensei had decided that the JKS would pay all expenses, including flights, hotel and food. We didn't have to do anything except facilitate the event and give them the profits.

We booked the whole of Crawley Sports Centre, which gave us the use of the massive sports hall, a dance studio and several squash courts. In reality, it wasn't quite so straightforward. We had wanted to organize a JKS championships, so we convinced the Headquarters that a seminar should be held on the Friday and Saturday and the championships on the Sunday. The Headquarters decided that instead of bringing all instructors, they would leave Takahashi Sempai and Yamada Sempai at home and bring Matsumura Sensei and Hashimoto Sensei instead. These two sensei were both 8th

dan, senior members of the executive board. However, they were not Kenshusei graduates and, being in their seventies, they lacked the gravitas that Takahashi Sempai and Yamada Sempai had in bucket loads. They also flew business class, along with Taguchi Sensei: a great business idea had been dashed by replacing the two most dynamic instructors with business class-flying septuagenarians.

The course made a huge loss, but it amounted to exactly what had been paid for said business-class tickets, so Peter and I never felt particularly guilty. Plus, teaching on one seminar we had Taguchi Sensei, Yumoto Sensei, Koyama Sempai, Sueki, the newly graduated Hirota and myself. Matsumura Sensei and Hashimoto Sensei walked around the massive dojo, adjusting people's stances, giving a 'well done' and 'good, good' on occasions and basically being Mr Miyagi-ish throughout. They were a huge hit. Hirota was awesome. He taught *Gojushiho-Dai*. I was teaching another class at the time, but I saw people come out of the dojo in awe, mouths agape. Like a tag team, Taguchi Sensei dazzled the first day, before tagging Yumoto Sensei who then further dazzled the second day. They were magicians. Sueki rocketed from one side of the dojo to the other. Powered by some invisible CIA pulse engine, he hurtled through time and space with devastating efficiency. Koyama Sempai answered the age-old question of what happens when an unstoppable force hits an immovable object. People bounced off him like ping-pong balls and his body mass, rooted to his suction-grip stance, proved the immovable object always wins.

It was finally my turn to teach the seniors. I was given the 4th dan and above group and about twenty-five karate-*ka* piled into a squash court. Peter joined them and saw the look on my face.

'Just do what you do best,' he said, stopping me at the entrance. 'They'll love it!'

I took a deep breath and walked in. Some people would say I was paranoid, I would call it insightful. I got the distinct impression they were looking at me with a 'go on, prove yourself if you can' attitude. I started with a few punches in front stance. Most had very little internal tension in their stance.

'Er ... I often see this problem,' I remember saying. I hated giving direct criticism – who am I to judge? I stood them up. 'Look, we need to lock in our stance when we drive forward. Think about it like this.' I jumped up, fairly high for me, then as I fell to the ground, snapped out my legs and locked into front stance. Without a wobble I held the floor. 'Do you see?' I had them. I went on to talk about hip-generated movement, using one's centre to transition in stance, rather than flailing about with arms and legs. It worked, and a decade later I can remember exactly what I taught and how I won them over – it was a great feeling.

The three days flew by and were a huge success. Over 250 karate-*ka* from all over the world had descended on an ugly part of London to train with the best of the JKS. A grading had been held on the Friday afternoon. Tor graded to 3rd dan and Peter re-graded to 5th dan, ratifying the grade he had received the year before. I was so deeply proud of both of them. Guus, on the other hand, seemed to pull a fast one. He was the same grade as Peter and we thought he had also decided to ratify his grade with Taguchi Sensei. However, when they lined up, Taguchi Sensei went down the line asking what rank people were grading for. Guus was last, just after Peter.

'And Guus. What grade?' Taguchi Sensei asked in his perfunctory English.

'6th dan,' Guus answered, as if it were the most natural thing in the world. Peter glanced at his friend. The grading commenced and by the end Guus was suddenly one of the most senior members of the JKS in Europe. How did that happen? thought more than one or two people. Similar to dynamics in any family or group, things went unsaid and were allowed to fester in the political subconscious of JKS Europe.

Post-training refreshments soon lead to late-night drinks, which gave way to new friends in the dojo the next morning. I made contact and re-established a connection with a huge number of instructors not only in the UK, but also from much farther afield. One chap, Felipe, had travelled from Rio de Janeiro. A talented, athletic instructor, he had liked what I did and asked me to come to Brazil to teach. I said yes immediately, bursting with excitement to tell Tor and Peter. But before I could, Felipe had fallen into conversation with Peter over a bottle of wine. I joined the chat midway through Peter suggesting that he and I travel over to teach. Felipe, unsure what to say, mumbled something about it being a great idea.

'Don't worry,' Peter added, picking up on Felipe's hesitation, 'we will do it for free, won't we Scott?' I nodded as I slumped back in my chair. 'Excellent!' he boomed as he meandered off to the toilet. Felipe looked at me.

'That's fine,' I said, 'if it is fine with you? Instead of paying me a salary, it will cover the cost of Peter's flight.'

'Are you sure?' Felipe looked at me, wondering why I had just thrown away my salary.

'Sometimes, in business, friendship is more important.' Actually I am sure I never said that – I was too drunk. But whatever I said, it was what I meant.

Monday morning we deposited the instructors at the

airport and made our way north to decompress for a day before returning to Ireland. It was a huge success, both in what we had achieved – a world-class karate seminar, putting both the JKS and the JKS GB & Ireland firmly on the map – and what we hadn't achieved. The competition was an unmitigated catastrophe. I had never run a championship before so took Peter's lead. However, it was a far cry from what I was used to, which were Japanese tournaments that ran on Swiss-precision timing. I learnt a lot that day, not only in category timing, competitor coordination and referee control, but also in conflict management, especially when the Palestinian group brought the whole arena to a halt when they refused to verify that their rather talented 6" 1" moustached fighter was actually appropriately placed in the 14 to 15-year male *kumite* section. It was a scene from a farce with all the wit replaced with aggression and all the slapstick with threats of violence to me and my family.

As we headed to Leicester the stress of the previous day dissipated. In the following weeks we would learn that the JKA had been spying on the event. Still in turmoil after the passing of Enoeda Sensei, the larger-than-life patriarchal figure who had defined Shotokan Karate not only in the UK, heading the Karate Union of Great Britain (KUGB), but also in Europe for over four decades, the JKA in Britain had split down the middle and the remaining Japan-loyal group struggled to maintain dominance. As a result, they followed the only path they knew – increasing control and tightening their grip on the membership. Many who attended the seminar received letters. If they committed that sort of crime again, they would be expelled from the group; these were men and women who had trained for decades with the JKA, and had shown loyalty and dedication that would put an ardent football fanatic to shame. They were threatened for simply wanting to train with Taguchi Sensei and Yumoto Sensei, who a decade before had been JKA Chief Instructor and JKA Grand Champion respectively.

Several months later Tor was travelling a lot with work. She had been staying in the south midlands and had decided to train with a local university. A week later she found herself in London, so rang the JKA head office to see where the nearest JKA club was.

'Who do you train with?'

'I am part of the JKS. I train with Scott Langley and Yumoto Sensei.'

'Who? I have never heard of them. Anyway, if you are not JKA, you can't train in any of our dojos,' came the stern response.

'Well, last week I trained with a university affiliated to you,' she naively mentioned. We heard later that the whole of the university, including over a hundred regular karate-loving undergraduates of varying grade and rank had been suspended, unable to grade or train. For us, this was a fantastic response. It didn't really matter if the JKA were responding to the break-up of the once dominant KUGB or the establishment of the JKS, or a bit of both. The only thing that mattered was how they were reacting. They, and other groups, became our best advertisement. All we had to do was teach good karate and be nice to people. It didn't take an organizational genius.

As we rolled into 2005, clubs in the UK and Ireland started to join. Generally they followed the same pattern: we would see one or two senior grades at a seminar I conducted or at one of the open events we held with a visiting Headquarters instructor. They would linger at the back of the dojo, sticking out like a sore thumb by not wanting to be seen. Next time their entourage would be larger. Then maybe that day or a few days later I would receive an email, asking if I would like to instruct at their dojo. Of course I would! And before long I would be sitting in a pub, post seminar, enjoying a pint with good people and they would mention affiliation.

'Of course,' I would say. 'I can send you all the information.' I would then give them the highlights of the structure: no dojo fee, individual membership fee (cheap in comparison to other groups), instructors eligible to become grading examiners from 3rd dan and cheap *kyu* grading registration fee – by the end of the small presentation most were already convinced. I hated the hard sell.

'This is a big decision, so please take your time. I would hate you to make a decision that you are not 100 per cent sure of. So I'll send you the info on Monday and if you have any questions, just let me know.' Most of the time I would receive an email by Tuesday saying they were in. This may have been a deliberately constructed soft-sell approach, but I hope to think it was also very genuine. I meant what I said, but I suppose as it initially gained results, my spiel became more refined. There are many truths to any story and this was no different.

The Japan trips continued in 2005 and 2006, and I also started to teach farther afield. In 2005 the connection I had made with Felipe paid dividend. Peter and I boarded a plane bound for Rio de Janeiro and I was filled with Christmas Eve-like excitement. Years before Ishii Sensei had made a similar teaching trip to the city and I was in awe at how his fame had spread across the world. Now I couldn't believe my career had reached such a level so quickly – albeit I was teaching for free.

After bisecting the north and south Atlantic, we eventually arrived in a technicolour paradise and spent a week soaking up the heat, scenery and sugar-cane alcohol. Felipe was the perfect host. Rapidly approaching forty, he was as lean and tanned as the teenagers he shared Ipanema Beach with during his early morning surfs. He showed us the sights, including the famous Sugarloaf Mountain topped with the impossibly large statue of Christ. However, we also got the inside story of this notoriously dangerous city. Getting closer than Felipe would have liked, he showed us the *favelas*, city slums that tumble down the hillsides like a mudslide of Crown paint. They looked amazing and seemed to inspire most of the art in the area. We were assured, however, that anyone venturing into these labyrinths would be mugged, raped, shot or decapitated – although the order in which it would happen was uncertain. We beat a hasty retreat, but felt perfectly safe under Felipe's guidance.

Eventually we had to do some work and made our way to a large naval base where Felipe's connections had secured one of the best facilities in the city. The course was busy and we were mostly well received. However, on seminars at that time there were always one or two attendees ready to give me a disapproving look and ignite my insecurities. This course was no different, as several members who had probably been training longer than I had been alive made certain judgmental sounds as I demonstrated various points. It was only later, when Felipe showed us a video from the year before of a very senior American-based, Japanese instructor who had taught in the same venue, that I realized the cause of such negative reactions. The previous seminar had been the culmination of several years of fundraising, whereby every member of the group, from white belt upwards, had paid weekly into the fund. Once the instructor's high fee, business-class plane ticket and five-star hotel could be covered, the seminar was organized. However, only 3rd dan instructors and above could attend. Karate-*ka* packed themselves into the crammed venue and were taught a variety of basic concepts, some of which were very dated. The Japanese instructor had been peerless for decades. This may have resulted in certain idiosyncratic principles being highlighted that were not completely congruent with what was now taught in Japan – our visit had certainly thrown the cat amongst the pigeons. However, despite this little hiccup, it was the highlight of 2005.

2006 was equally interesting and busy. In the early spring I was invited to the Ukraine, and after several flights found myself in the idyllic Crimea. Then and now it conjures up images of violence and war, but I timed my visit perfectly and taught the joint camp of a Russian and Ukrainian karate group. It was a bit of a mismatch, with the two groups being predominantly sports-karate based, only really interested in how to score points and cheat at *kata*. I tried to plunder the far corners of my mind and the internet to come up with something they would like. It seemed to work and they were happy with my efforts.

But I was far too distracted with my surroundings to worry about the fact that I was teaching a superficial and insincere type of karate. We ventured into Balaklava as I tried to remember my A Level history of the region. Nestled in this beautiful Black Sea port was the Russian submarine naval base. One side of the natural dock was a sheer cliff face and excavated into it was a large man-made cave, half submerged by the sea. It could have been lifted from any Bond film and I desperately wanted to investigate the cavernous interior, where I was convinced a supervillain's private army prepared for world dominance.

We wandered into a store to buy some water and walked straight into a Cold War movie from the 1950s. Dusty shelves showed off the occasional tatty can of beans or curly, unidentifiable vegetable. I went to take a photo but was chased out of the shop by a fat and furious Russian-speaking woman; I am sure she was wielding her broom at me. It was hilarious and at the same time frightening that I was only a few hours from home – this part of Ukraine definitely wasn't part of Western Europe.

By the spring of 2006 my dojo locations had reached maximum capacity. With 150 members, my nine hours of teaching a week produced a great wage and my weekend work had grown to in excess of twenty courses per year. In June 2005 Tor moved over to Dublin. She had given up thinking my Irish dream might fail, hoping I would return to England. In April 2006 we were married in Disneyworld – by Mickey Mouse.

On our return, two incidents in the dojo changed the course of my business. Monday afternoons I taught at LA Fitness. One day a man popped his head in as I commanded and conducted the movements of twenty *dogi*-clad kids. I thought he was a prospective parent and after the class I met him outside and went into sales mode.

'So, how much do you charge per class?'

'Actually it's €22 per month … the first two weeks are free,' I beamed.

'How many kids do you have in a class?'

'A maximum of twenty with one instructor, two instructors if there are more.' Gayle had become my part-time paid assistant.

'How long have you been teaching here?'

'Er, three years.' This wasn't the normal series of questions that prospective parents ask.

'How much do you pay for studio rent?' My quizzical look was enough to spur him on. 'I'm the new manager. How much do you pay for rent?'

'€20 per hour,' I mumbled.

'Okay, we're just looking at the business structure. I'll be in touch next week.' Which he certainly did. They tripled my rent.

The following week the secretary of Rathgar Parish Hall met me as I was about to begin my three-class Thursday evening. 'Scott, great news – we've just been given a grant to refurbish the entire centre.'

'That's great!' I said, looking around the drab, badminton court-sized hall, which featured an amateur operatic stage at one end and an abandoned sandpit at the other.

'Oh, but we'll be shut for a year,' she added, almost as an afterthought, as she exited through ill-fitting, draughty swing doors.

I had seventy members training on Thursday evenings. At LA Fitness I had two profitable classes, but not enough to withstand a €480 monthly rent bill. As a business it was unsustainable. I was vulnerable to the whims of the local parish council or some new, gung-ho management team, wanting to shake things up. Tor convinced me that I had to find my own dojo.

Within a month I had found an old garage in Ranelagh, a location that was equidistant from most of my existing venues. In June I signed the five-year lease and we set about transforming the oil-stained shell of a building into a quintessentially Japanese dojo. By the summer of 2006 I had built up a strong core of friends and students. Maz still played a huge part in my life, both in the dojo and outside. But in the four years I had been there many other characters entered my life.

John, a senior figure within the Irish karate world, was one of the first black belts to turn up at my dojo and show support. He had an eclectic karate background, formed by having worked all over the world. He was now back in Dublin and trained daily with me – he was tough and funny and I was glad he had come to find me. Fergus had a successful dojo on the northside of Dublin. He was one of the guys that sniffed about for a while and then jumped on board. He had great technique, trained hard and had a fantastic sense of humour. Suddenly these senior karate-*ka* wanted to help. John was a project manager for a huge construction company. He knew every chippy, sparky and bricky in the whole of Dublin – not that I knew what these were, but I gathered we needed them to build a dojo. Fergus was a taxi driver, but had a passion for karate, so I was never alone during that summer as he, through the day, and John, in the evenings, slowly helped to build my new home. I was deeply grateful for their effort, guidance and support during a nerve-racking time.

I had decided to keep the two farthest classes running, but had abandoned all the others and brought them to the dojo. At the same time I had signed lots of legal documents that put the St Killian's commitment permanently in the pile labelled 'small potatoes'. If it didn't work out I would be ruined. I had given away prime-time slots in prime venues around the prime neighbourhoods of south Dublin. Just before we opened I spoke to James, a 6th dan who consistently came to my Monday evening class. He was the head of his own Shotokan group in Ireland and had been a great fighter in his day. His attendance in my class possibly offered inspiration for his own seminars.

'Scott, I wish you well,' he said, as the conversation turned to the new schedule in the new full-time dojo. 'But it'll never work.'

Oh, really? I thought.

As the summer drew to a close, friends, in-laws, students and students' parents lent a hand to make sure the venue was ready on time. One student, Gavan, whose company specialized in flooring, had a top-quality martial-arts floor 'system' imported from Germany. Charging me well below cost price, he then worked through the night in order to have it fitted for opening day. I was and still am staggered and flabbergasted by the level and depth of people's generosity.

But in late August, as I drove to the dojo to start another day of hard labour, Koyama Sempai called me. 'Scott, I have some bad news. Taguchi Sensei has died.'

The funeral was scheduled for the week after, Friday 1 September. My dojo's opening party was on Saturday 2 September. I had to attend the funeral, there was no question about it. I looked online and found I could fly Wednesday 30 August, arriving on the Thursday.

I checked in to a six-*tatami* room at Kimi *Ryokan*, which may have been the very same room I stayed in on my return to Japan after my knee injury almost a decade before. I met Tom and Hiro and drank in Tengu until very late. It was as if I had never been away. Friday morning I made my way to the shrine and with the karate world present, we said goodbye to Taguchi Sensei. There would be political ramifications from Taguchi Sensei's passing, but at the time it was just a sad moment, cut short by my 10 p.m. flight back to Ireland. I left the wake prematurely, but explained my reasoning to everyone I thought should know. I jumped on the Narita Express and my less-than-48-hour stay in Japan was over. I landed at 1 p.m. the following day in Dublin and dashed to the dojo for the 2 p.m. start of the party. It was a crazy couple of days, but I arrived to a purpose-built dojo, with all the edges trimmed, corners brushed and shiny bits polished. Tor, my parents-in-law, Gavin, John, Fergus, Gayle, Maz and many other students had worked tirelessly to make sure it was ready on time. Seventy or so students of varying ages turned up at the allocated time, and a newly opened sushi restaurant from just around the corner supplied the food. I had brought back ample *sake* and grapefruit sour from my jaunt to Tokyo and a great party ensued.

The JKS now had a new direction. Yumoto Sensei would become the head and that would mean everyone would be moving up. My dojo was open for business – the first professionally run, full-time dojo in Ireland. JKS GB & Ireland now had a Hombu Dojo (headquarters) of its own. We were starting to make waves within the karate scene in the British Isles and punching well above our weight. And my international career was going well, so well in fact that I could no longer sustain teaching so many hours through the week and then teaching at least two weekends per month, sometimes three. Change was inevitable. For now, however, I enjoyed the culmination of what I had worked for. Four years earlier I had left Japan with a very precise idea of what I wanted – this, however, went well beyond anything I could have dreamt of.

SIX

The death of Taguchi Sensei in 2006 rippled throughout the karate world. These were the early days of Facebook, but the karate community had soon learnt to master its true purpose: gossip. Yumoto Sensei was only 7th dan. With several 8th dan instructors above him, speculation grew as to who would be made head. Some suggested that William Blunt Sensei, an 8th dan from South Africa and only non-Japanese instructor to attain such a rank, may be given the top job; others suggested Hiro Watabe from Hokkaido, an 8th dan who knew all the *koten* (ancient) *kata* that Taguchi Sensei taught. It was all nonsense. We knew, well at least those who knew anything, that Yumoto Sensei would be made Chief Instructor – there was no question about it. It wasn't a matter of rank or length of service, they were the superficial elements of a karate instructor. Yumoto Sensei was the most senior member of the Headquarters. He was Technical Director and technically the best in the JKS, if not the world. Of course he would be made Chief Instructor.

Actually he wasn't. He remained Technical Director. There would be no Chief Instructor. The executive – Matsumura Sensei, Hashimoto Sensei and various other senior members of the JKS (all Japanese) – decided that there would only be one *Shuseki Shihan* (World Chief Instructor). Taguchi Sensei had founded the association and he would, for evermore, be the chief. I could see their point but I didn't like it. The

JKS was more than Taguchi Sensei. Yes, he had been the first Chief Instructor, but the group was made up of many great instructors supported by an even greater number of seniors, teaching a much greater number of affiliates and their students. Besides, throughout the six years of the JKS's birth and growth, Taguchi Sensei had been duplicitously supporting and developing the TBKA. As much as the JKS was more than Taguchi Sensei, it seemed that Taguchi Sensei had been more than just the JKS.

But this was, once and for all, put to bed. Shima Sempai, who, not so secretly, ran the TBKA from Taguchi Sensei's import-export company in Shimbashi, sent a message to all TBKA affiliates: they must affiliate directly to the JKS or leave. Ishii Sensei left. Well he didn't really leave, he announced that he was now Chief Instructor of the TBKA and took some of the affiliates with him. Others joined the JKS. I was glad. The TBKA would slowly be marginalized as they had become yet another international organization monopolized and dictated by one person. There may have been depth with Ishii Sensei, but no breadth. The JKS kept its form and moved forward.

2007 was the fiftieth anniversary of the passing of Funakoshi Sensei, the founder of Shotokan Karate. It was decided that the JKS would hold our world championships in Okinawa and have a ceremony commemorating the occasion. So, despite the growing popularity of the *Kangeiko* trips to Japan, this year I decided we would take in Okinawa. I offered a multi-choice trip: people could come along to the mainland first, initially recovering from jet lag in Hakone, then spending time with Yokose Sensei, before heading to the Headquarters. Then we would fly south to Okinawa where we would meet the people who opted for choice B, spend a week in Okinawa, and compete in the World Championships. The

JKS GB & Ireland had grown significantly, and the group size had swelled to thirty-three members, twenty-one opting for choice A and the rest heading over for the second week.

I was nervous about coordinating such an expedition. The total cost was in excess of €50,000. It wasn't as if I was ABTA-approved either: if I fucked up, it would be on my head. It took months to prepare, but by the time Yumoto Sensei arrived in the UK for his now annual spring visit, all bookings had been made and I went over my plan meticulously, hoping he would spot any potential flaw. He didn't and was very pleased to hear I would be bringing so many people. Apparently, we were the third-biggest team behind Japan and South Africa. Japan, of course, would dominate the event. South Africa, with its rich karate history and being headed up by William Sensei would also vie for dominance. However, JKS GB & Ireland, headed up by a mere 4th dan, having only been established four and a half years previously, would be a large force too. Whether we could win any medals was a different matter altogether!

Just after Easter 2007 my group found themselves bound for Narita. Making our way to Hakone first was a great idea. The group bonded and relaxed as spring in Japan swept through the archipelago with a flourish of cherry blossom. We managed to catch the back end of it and although far from its potential magnificence, it was enough to impress the assembled karate-*ka*. From Hakone we travelled to Yokose Sensei and, as previous years, were treated to an extravaganza of Japanese hospitality. This time, with our swollen numbers, they had set up several mini marquees along the side of the local river and in the warm spring sunshine we ate, drank and partied the whole day. Waves of Yokose Sensei's students and friends came to chat, entertain and be entertained by the lumbering *gaijin*. In the evening, as we decamped back at his dojo and were expecting a welcome retreat to our homestays, Yokose Sensei told me to get everyone to follow him. We wandered the back streets of his local town, which could have been lifted from any ninja movie set and, turning a corner, entered an ancient-looking temple. With fairy lights and electric lanterns draped throughout and long trestle tables making neat lines in the open space, a festival was in full swing.

The arrival of nearly two-dozen *gaijin* created a bit of a stir. Tor and a few of the other girls on the trip were treated like royalty by the elderly gentlemen, who, like us, seemed to have been drinking all day. They could have veered into the realms of lechery but instead they were charming, charismatic and fun. One old chap had a smidgeon of English and was endlessly harangued by his compatriots as they got him to translate (rather poorly) their many questions and comments. I stood most of the evening with Yokose Sensei and some of his seniors; after all my time in Japan I had had my fill of 'Where are you from?', 'Why are you here?' and 'Can you use chopsticks?'-type questions. My group was lapping it up. I scanned the open area of the temple. At one end some of the older ladies were teaching the younger members of our group a traditional Japanese dance. The *gaijin* ladies were still being charmed by the charismatic retirees and in another area the rest were playing traditional games – one of which was trying to catch goldfish with a rice-paper sieve. When we left, everyone, Japanese and *gaijin*, was beaming with delight and it was by far the best day of any trip we had had, thanks again to Yokose Sensei.

The following day we made our way to Tokyo and the Headquarters. I steeled myself as we drew closer and my automatic defence mechanism kicked in. As I entered and warmed up it seemed that, for once, my psychosis was justified. The only people at the dojo were Sueki, Hirota and Koga (who, with Mark, had just entered the Instructors' Course). There was a certain chill in the air. They never said anything, but if I had had spidery sensors, they would have been tingling.

The class started, like it had every time I'd been there, but something was off. Halfway through the basics, for some unknown reason, I glanced over at the instructors' name board. My name had been taken off. A special section of instructor graduates living abroad listed only three of us. From right to left our names and respective countries were noted: Nakaya (Canada), Koyama (France), Scott (Ireland). Now there were only two names. As I marched up and down the dojo, Sueki trying to kill off my guys, my mind raced as to what this meant. Was I no longer an Instructors' Course graduate? I had no answer.

Before long Sueki called for us to pair up. Everyone dashed for the blood- and sweat-soaked mitts at the side of the dojo and we faced partners. Considering most of the guys would be competing in less than a week, I presumed it would be light sparring. However, within seconds Koga had taken his first *gaijin* scalp.

'Okay, change!' Sueki barked out the command.

Again Koga dropped someone else as Sueki and Hirota watched passively. Peter looked over to me. I knew what Sueki was doing. It is a punishment routine that our sempai and their sempai before them had played out and I wanted no part of it. Sueki commanded us to change again and I bowed out and walked to Sueki. Enough was enough.

'Koga pair up with Scott.'

He was directing his *kohai*. Really? He wanted Koga to try

it on with me? I couldn't believe what I was hearing. 'Enough!'

'What?' He jerked round and looked at me.

'Sueki, ENOUGH!' He scrutinized me with eyes that I had not seen since the dark days of the Instructors' Course. His glazed expression continued as Koga found another victim to maul. I continued to stare back. Then a glimmer of himself appeared and he called a halt to the proceedings.

'Okay, *kata*,' he called out and we finished the session in a subdued hush. The class ended, lesson learnt. I got my guys to change quickly and we left.

'See you in Okinawa,' I said as I left the dojo. I was in no mood for normal Japanese pleasantries and gratitude on our departure.

Several days later the new, larger group made our way to the Okinawan Budokan, a palace dedicated to all things martial, for the ceremony commemorating the life of Funakoshi Sensei. He had been sent by the karate groups in Okinawa to demonstrate the art on the mainland in 1917. As a high-school teacher, he had been the most educated and sophisticated out of the mixed bag of top karate-*ka* on the islands. He had done well. In less than fifty years, karate, especially what would develop into his brand of karate, would traverse the world and become the most widespread form of martial arts. And so we found ourselves celebrating such an achievement with a beautifully engraved monolith. The area was packed with JKS national teams from around the world. I tried to keep my guys together as I bounced from one '*yoroshiku*' to another 'hey, how're you doing'. Eventually I found Takahashi Sempai.

'*Osu*, Sensei. How are you?' It had been a year since we had last met and I was pleased to see him. It wasn't reciprocated.

'Why did you go to Yokose Sensei's dojo?'

'Er …' I didn't know what to say. 'We go there every year, Sensei.'

'Yokose Sensei is a Teikyo University connection. If you go to his dojo, you *must* tell us first!' He was really angry, angrier than I had ever seen him.

'*Osu*. I understand.' I didn't, but what else could I say? He stormed off.

Out of all my seniors at the Headquarters, I felt closest to Takahashi Sempai. We were more similar than either of us liked to admit. However, I had broken our bond all those years before when I had refused to participate in Instructors' Training.

I stood there in shock. Koyama Sempai had seen the incident and came over.

'Is that why my name has been taken off the board?' He nodded. 'But I explained my plan to Yumoto Sensei two months ago. They knew I was going to Yokose Sensei's dojo first. Logistically we couldn't have done it any other way.' I was trying to justify my actions as if what I had done was in any way inappropriate.

'Yumoto Sensei knew?' Koyama Sempai was a little taken aback.

'Yeah, he knew everything. He is the head of Teikyo, I always let him know our plans.'

'Don't worry.' Koyama Sempai said reassuringly. 'It's just a short-term punishment. Maybe six months at most.'

I was deeply upset. Yet again, Yumoto Sensei had failed to support me. He must have remembered the conversation. He must have had a discussion with Takahashi Sempai. There must have been a moment when he could have stepped in and prevented Takahashi Sempai from taking my name from the board. But just like the situation with Tamata-san several years ago, he decided to sit back and let it happen.

I had been out of Japan for almost as long as I had been in Japan. The first few years following my graduation I had seemed to ride a wave of support and good faith, but things were changing. Takahashi Sempai had been made head of the international department of the JKS and took control of managing people throughout the world, but he was more unilateral than United Nations about things. In a private moment another sempai voiced his concern: Yamada Sempai had been put in charge of domestic affiliates, and, combined with Takahashi Sempai's role, they would be like two Rottweilers protecting Yumoto Sensei.

I eventually saw Yumoto Sensei, who was charming and pleasant, as if he knew nothing of my alleged *faux pas* with Yokose Sensei. Yokose Sensei had heard of the situation and sought me out to give some fatherly advice.

'You must tell Yumoto Sensei your plans.'

'I did, Sensei. Two months ago!' I felt someone senior must know the truth.

'Oh … okay. Well it'll only be short term. Don't worry.' So the consensus all round was just to shut up and take the punishment.

At the following welcoming party I hopped from one table to another, chatting to seniors from different countries. Some I had known since I was a kid, training on courses with Ishii Sensei. They had come to the JKS through the same route as me. Others were traditional JKA members, who had arrived at this spot after supporting Taguchi Sensei when the initial split happened; either way, I knew who they were and they knew who I was. At one point I stumbled across Murakami Sensei from the Shotokan Karate International Federation (SKIF), another Shotokan group. He had been invited along to teach on the seminar in the coming days and to celebrate Funakoshi Sensei's life. I had trained with him over a decade earlier when he had assisted Kanazawa Sensei in the UK. He was standing by himself, so I thought I would go over to say hello.

'*Osu*, Sensei. My name is …'

'*Osu*, Scott Sensei. Good to see you.' Wow, he knew me!

'Good to see you too, Sensei. I just wanted to say I trained with you ten years ago and I am looking forward to training with you again tomorrow.' I genuinely was. He was the SKIF equivalent of Takahashi Sempai: young, dynamic, talented.

'I think I remember – it was Blackpool, wasn't it?' I nodded, in awe of his memory. 'I read your articles in *Shotokan Karate Magazine* – they are very good,' he added. I beamed as we continued this mutual appreciation society for a while until someone else wanted an audience. With a '*Yoroshiku Onegashimasu*' I departed, elated by the encounter, which was in stark contrast to the conversations I had with my sempai. It took a relative stranger to remind me I was at least doing something right.

The party continued. As I social-butterflied around the room I kept noticing Takahashi Sempai glancing my way. Was I being paranoid? Maybe the first few times, but the trend continued. I don't know if it was my normal Japan stress, the alcohol, a reaction to having my name taken off the board or a genuine perception of the new reality. He seemed to be watching every interaction I had with the international members of his congregation. He didn't seem to like it and it started to dawn on me. Was I becoming too popular? My dojo had swelled to in excess of 250 members. The JKS GB & Ireland now had over fifty affiliated dojos. I was teaching weekend seminars twice a month and the types of seminars I was invited to had grown in prestige. My personal promotion plan had got my foot in the door to some big national groups and my teaching style had made me a regular on national technical seminars throughout Europe and farther afield. This whole de-boarding fiasco obviously wasn't about me going to Yokose Sensei's dojo. I wondered if Takahashi Sempai was ever so slightly jealous of my success. But why? He was awesome, one of the best in the world. I was a westerner teaching traditional karate in a Japanophile-dominated culture. He was a karate master personified. I was a *gaijin*, forever destined to not quite belong, no matter where I settled. He oozed talent and skill. I compensated for my challenges with wit and charm. He had the best of the Japanese karate system as his foundations. I had a chatty disposition and a few well-timed quips as mine. I was and always would be in awe of him, so where was the problem?

The week in Okinawa was fantastic. It was Japan without the hustle and bustle, without the formality and conformity, without the rush hour trains and pushy sempai. Kokusai Dori, the main drag in the capitol, Naha, was a long straight road filled with an assortment of trinket shops, fast-food joints, bars, restaurants, markets and the most wonderful array of people. It always seemed packed, no matter what time of day. We had two free days to explore this tropical paradise. The locals were pleasant, warm and friendly – Tokyo may be the most welcoming of mega-cities but Naha was just the most welcoming of places.

We visited Shuri Castle, the seat of power of this once-medieval island chain dynasty. It was also the birthplace of *Shuri-Te*, one of original forms of *Okinawan-Te* (Okinawan Hand). We then literally crossed the road from the castle and wandered around Tomari, a labyrinth of rice-paper-clad homes and shops, selling all things tropically oriental.

Tomari is the birthplace of *Tomari-Te,* the working-class rival to *Shuri-Te*. It was easy to imagine the tough, rough and poor street brawlers living in the shadow of the castle, developing their own brand of fighting, looking across the road to the upper classes and their unique style and thinking, 'Those guys are wimps. They're shit!' whilst the elite looked on with disgust thinking, 'Look at those oafs. That's just brute force and ignorance!'

However, like any great rivalry, it produced two distinct styles of *Okinawan-Te* that Funakoshi Sensei would eventually study and later combine to produce Shotokan Karate. Shoto was Funakoshi Sensei's pen-name and *kan* means place or palace. So Shotokan was just the original name of his dojo. Karate now means Empty Hand, but this was changed from the original meaning, Chinese Hand, so-called because the oafs from Tomari and the toffs from Shuri originally learnt their deadly moves from Chinese sailors who in turn had learnt their moves from the fighting monks of Shaolin. Japan may have very few inventions under its belt, but the Japanese are excellent innovators and karate is one of their prized possessions.

After walking through the living history of Okinawan Karate, I left my merry band to wander the markets of Kokusai Dori so I could decide which of the many restaurants we would dine in that evening. The choice was varied and wide. However, in the evenings our numbers would swell to forty or so *gaijin*.

Certain members of the Norwegian, Swedish and German teams had decided to tag along, knowing that my Japanese allowed them to gain access to the best of Okinawa. I would find an interesting venue and negotiate a good price for a *gaijin*-friendly set menu with *nomihou-dai*. One night we dined at a Teppanyaki restaurant that served the freshest and most delicate of seafood, at the end of which the chef presented prawn crackers actually made from the exoskeletons of the crustaceans we had just eaten – they were surprisingly delicious! Another night we ate in a private *tatami* room whilst a shy, smiling girl shuffled in to serve plate after plate of steaming food. All the while a preposterously small septuagenarian sat in the corner playing a *Shamisen*, the high-pitched, ear-drum-piercing Japanese guitar. When the food and entertainment were over, Simon, who had made a welcome return to Japan after nearly twenty years, was convinced to get up and 'do a bit'. A truly professional comedian, he bounded up and delivered a thirty-minute set of pure genius. At one point several punters from the floor below politely knocked on the door. They were curious as to why the wood- and rice-paper building was shaking with laughter.

Our group would then split, some going home, others going to a *sake* bar, which we were sure had been lifted from the set of *Kill Bill*. Some wandered down Kokusai Dori, trying to convince others to buy the local spirit, which had a dead snake fermenting in the pickle. Others went to the African-themed bar just below our hotel. The bar had alcoves dug out of the wall where groups of two or four could sit, cocooned in their drunkenness. The owner, an anglophile, was delighted that for a week he could practise his English with the endless procession of *gaijin* that stumbled into his bar. I had never been to Okinawa when I lived in Japan and I now regretted that I hadn't.

The training camp and competition was scheduled over three days. On the first day over 200 karate-*ka* packed into the largest of the dojos in the Budokan. Tsuyama Sensei, infamous for producing some of the best JKA instructors through Takushoku University, kicked off proceedings and did a splendid job representing the JKA on this multi-organizational camp.

The class was basic but tough, made almost unbearable by the heat, but Tsuyama Sensei was a legend, so just to be in the same room as him was enough for most people there. Murakami Sensei followed and taught a well-thought-out class in perfect English (the only one to do so). I think Takahashi Sempai had the edge on him in terms of dynamic speed and sharpness of technique, but what Murakami Sensei lacked in explosiveness he more than made up for in intelligence and intellect. Yumoto Sensei brought the proceedings to a close with a classic lesson of his: hip snap, suppleness of joints, total body action – he was a physical genius, able to do anything with his body after decades of relentless dedication to hard training. We all walked out of the dojo dripping with sweat, happy and ready for the two days ahead.

Despite the multi-organizational approach to the laying of the monument and training camp, the competition was a JKS-only affair. The event had now moved into the massive auditorium on the Budokan. With twelve matted areas perfectly laid out ready for the event, I had been assigned as part of the refereeing team on one of them. I wished my guys good luck and made my way, suited and booted, into the wonderfully air-conditioned stadium. What followed was a perfectly orchestrated two-day affair. The standard was marvellous: Japan, of course, dominated the medal podium, but their level was undeniably the best. Refereeing such an event is a pleasant experience. There were twice as many referees per area than were actually needed, which was just as well, as I was being asked to the head table to make regular announcements in English. By the second day I made my excuses to my area's senior and just sat at the head table – I don't know why I wasn't assigned there in the first place. Actually I do know; I was needed to translate. I had a sinking feeling about this dramatic turn of events. Thankfully, Takahashi Sempai never said anything when he saw I had repositioned myself.

I was also called upon to sort out certain issues arising from all the foreign teams. There was a constant stream of queries that had to be addressed, but unlike when I lived in Japan and had the pressure of competing as well, this was fine – I was happy to help. Unfortunately, halfway through the first day Takahashi Sempai came and told me to sort out William Blunt, who had apparently walked off like a petulant child. I found this strange: he was a seventy-year-old 8th dan. I eventually found him lurking in the coffee shop of the stadium.

'Sensei, is everything okay?'

'I've been sitting at my allocated area all morning and no one has said a word to me. I'm being completely ignored!' He wasn't being petulant, he was angry. He had sat all morning and no one had used him to referee, just leaving the solitary *gaijin* alone. I looked at the event brochure to see who was allocated to his area.

'Er, Sensei … you are the chief referee of that mat. You are in charge.' I thought for a second. 'Are you sure they are not just waiting for your direction?' He looked surprised. I took him back to his area, found someone I knew and explained the situation. He confirmed what I thought had happened. William Sensei hadn't taken control of the area so they just got on with it. However, no one had told William Sensei he was in control, expecting him to read the Japanese for 'chief referee'. It was crazy. If this was Takahashi Sempai's *modus operandi* for dealing with international affiliates, God help us.

The event came to a close and most of the teams bundled into the large bar located by the Budokan. Themed like a tree house, with an elevator tower as trunk and two floors perched on top making up the bulk of the tree, JKS GB & Ireland team members crushed together as we tried to decompress after the intensive few days. One of our members had done exceedingly well.

'Guys, come in, listen up.' I tried to get all of our squad together. 'I would like to say well done to every single one of you, you have made Peter Sensei and I very proud. One person in particular is going home with a gold medal,' there was a cheer from all round, 'a gold medal that he won on his birthday!' There was a greater cheer that rippled through the growing crowd. 'So I would like to congratulate the birthday boy becoming Veteran Kata World Champion – Fergus O'Keane!' A huge '*Ooosssuuu*!' reverberated around the tree house.

Fergus beamed as he should have done. He had trained hard two or three mornings a week and attended every seminar since joining the JKS two years earlier. He had spent the previous quarter of a century being told to do karate harder, faster and stronger by visiting UK instructors, but now he was absorbing this new approach of body mechanics like a sponge. The gold medal was hard-earned but well-deserved.

Shortly after, we decamped to a less crowded *izakaya* and the JKS GB & Ireland team had one last drink before we hit our futon. Peter called everyone to attention and asked for 'Best & Worst' of the trip – it was now a tradition. When it got to my turn I simply said: 'The worst part was when I saw that my name had been taken from the board … the best part was when I realized that my name being there no longer mattered.' There was a resounding '*Ooosssuuu*!' and we called it a night. The next day we packed, said our goodbyes and made the long journey back to Europe. I left Japan with a strange resignation. For such a long time it had been my second home, accommodating my oriental alter ego. I boarded the plane a little lighter, having lost something intangible. The sinking feeling was still present, but was it loss, fear, pride, resilience, defiance? Or all of the above?

During the conversation I had had with Yumoto Sensei two months before Okinawa, talk had turned to karate rank. 'What grade are you, Scott? 4th dan? When did you grade? Five years ago? Okay, you should grade this year.'

'*Osu*, Sensei!' I had been delighted to have been given the nod by Yumoto Sensei.

In July 2007 I travelled to Belgium where Yumoto Sensei was conducting a seminar. It was fun to attend a weekend camp without having to worry about looking after instructors or organizing schedules. In hindsight, I should have worried. Yumoto Sensei was told to teach for six hours per day and he was left alone during lunch and dinner. I couldn't do anything about his schedule, but I could at least make sure he had company when he ate. Over lunch the first day I asked if I should grade over the weekend.

'Why? When did you grade to 4th dan?' came the reply. No Sensei, this isn't me asking if I could grade, I am here because you told me to take the test, I wanted to say. Instead I answered the question as if we had never had our earlier conversation.

'Oh, okay. Try then,' came the reply. I walked away

from the table rubbing my head. A student doesn't ask his sensei to grade, it just wasn't done. Despite other seniors in Europe slowly creeping up and overtaking me on the grading ladder, even people who had joined the group well after I had returned from Japan, I had never pushed myself to be promoted. But yet again Yumoto Sensei had inconveniently forgotten our exchange and I now came across as the arrogant *gaijin* endlessly looking for a higher grade.

I graded the next day. Like any senior examination one must fight and perform two *kata*: one the candidate choses themselves (their best *kata*) and one that the examiner choses (any of the twenty-six Shotokan *kata*). I made one small mistake in the *kata* I was given to perform and failed the test. Before and after I have seen many people make far bigger mistakes, even in *kata* that they had chosen themselves. They are often overlooked or at the very least given a second chance to perform it correctly. I wasn't. Yumoto Sensei made no comment on my failure except to say that as a Headquarters instructor, only perfection was passable. In that case, I thought, maybe he should put my name back on the board.

That summer things continued to go well for the group and my dojo. We had had another massive influx of students to over 350 members. Fergus had started to teach part-time and with his own dojo on the northside of the city, he was able to quit his taxi-driver job and become a full-time instructor. I employed another friend to assist me in my ever-expanding classes, which meant I could leave the dojo anytime I wanted and know my classes would be covered. Although it happened organically, I found myself with the perfect set up.

To celebrate, I decided to treat myself. When I was a kid we had a family friend, the head gear-box mechanic for the

Lotus Formula One team. He had given me all the Lotus team uniform and I had been in love with the cars ever since. I had spoken to Peter about going to the UK to buy a second-hand car and asked him to help source one. He had eagerly agreed, being a bit of a petrol head, but that summer I went to the only dealership in Ireland and brought myself a brand-new Elise. I rang Peter to give him the good news.

'Scott, I always respect someone who is willing to pay that much for a car. Congratulations,' he said, obviously pleased for me. 'I didn't realize you were doing that well, though,' he added as an afterthought.

Two months later Takahashi Sempai visited Ireland for his annual gig for the JKS GB & Ireland. The first evening I collected him in my new car. He came out of the hotel and gawped. 'Okay, let's go!' he said with far more irritation than I expected. He slid into the car and never mentioned it at all for the entire weekend. As I revved, swerved and propelled us through the streets of Dublin his irritation seemed to increase. It had been decided that I would perform my *kata* over the weekend in front of Takahashi Sempai in order to re-grade for 5th dan. He seemed in a frightful mood the entire time, so I was loath to bring it up. Finally, on the Sunday afternoon after everyone had left, Peter finally reminded him.

'Okay, do the *kata*.' He pointed to the empty dojo. I did as commanded, this time not making the small mistake. He then began to point out other mistakes I had made in my performance. They weren't mistakes, just differences in interpretation. He saw it one way, I was taught another.

With an 'oh, do you mean like this?' I performed the *kata* again with his interpretation. He was still a feared sempai, but I'd done a lot of growing up in the last five years.

'You have to work on your *kata* and do it properly.'

I thought I just had done it correctly – his 'correctly', but Takahashi Sempai was having none of it. I was translating for Peter who was becoming increasingly agitated.

'Has he passed or failed?' Peter butted in, knowing that Takahashi Sempai could understand.

'Okay, pass,' he muttered grudgingly. It was a far cry from the celebratory occasion of my last grading.

That evening we had a subdued dinner and on the way back to the hotel I arranged a collection time to take him to the airport.

'Sensei, your flight is at 7.30 a.m.?'

'Yes. Collect me at 5 a.m.'

I did just that. However, when we got to the airport, his flight was actually at 5.30 a.m. He had missed it and would also miss the connecting flight. There was nothing we could do. I drove him back to my apartment. He was livid.

'*Shou ga nai*.' I said – it can't be helped.

'*Shou ga naku nai*!' came the terse response – he begged to differ.

Whose fault was it? I am not sure. I booked the flights, but had then forwarded him all the booking information. He had it at hand as he was flying home. I had asked him if it was 7.30 a.m. and he had confirmed it as being so. But in his eyes it was my fault and I had to get my credit card out and buy him a whole new flight. He left the next day, still angry, without a word of thanks. I joked with Peter that at least he didn't charge me the extra day's salary – at this point I wouldn't have put anything past him. On his first trip he had been friendly, accommodating, compliant, funny, charming and awesome. Four years later and he was irritable, demanding, uncooperative – and still awesome. It would be the last of his trips to the JKS GB & Ireland for a long time.

*

The next time I spoke to Takahashi Sempai was in the spring of 2008 when I called him with good news. 'Sensei, I have great news! JKA Scotland have left *en masse* and joined us!' I was ecstatic. Stewart Andrews was the high-profile head of the JKA north of the border. For over five years we had failed to make any impact outside the Republic of Ireland and England, but after a series of short phone calls we suddenly had the whole of the JKA-affiliated Scottish group join us. It was fantastic news and really affirmed what Peter and I had been doing. I was delighted to personally give Takahashi Sempai the good news.

'That isn't your decision! You aren't a Headquarters instructor. You can't decide who does and doesn't join the JKS!' I was glad to be sitting down.

'But Sensei …' I was reeling. 'We have had over fifty dojos join JKS GB & Ireland in the last five years and I never had to ask permission before.'

'This is a different county – Scotland is a different country!'

'Well, not really. Yes, it is, but no it isn't …' I went on to explain that there is a border, but it is open. And they have their own government, but only for certain domestic issues and we share a joint government based in Westminster. We also share the same passport and we are all British, citizens of the United Kingdom. Try explaining that in Japanese when your sempai is screaming down the phone at you. The conversation didn't go well. Apparently, when it came to passing – or failing – exams, I was a Headquarters instructor. When it came to deciding which dojos could join my group, I wasn't. The Venn diagram of my situation, responsibilities and position was very complicated.

The call ended with a general acceptance that they

could be provisional members for now until a time when a Headquarters instructor could meet them and decide. It was crazy, irrational, absurd. After years of hard work, Peter and I felt vindicated by such a large, legitimate group choosing us. They knew the JKS through what we had been doing. In fact our website was getting hits from all over the world, and it was a regular occurrence for me to get international enquiries regarding affiliation to the JKS. The JKS Japan website was still mostly in Japanese and still in the Stone Age of the internet world. Our site was current and in English. I responded to questions with the general brushstrokes of what JKS affiliation entailed and would then pass them up the line to the Headquarters for further action. Invariably I would get a follow-up email from the same group several weeks later saying they had heard nothing from Japan. I would repeat the appeal to the gods and weeks later I would receive another increasingly desperate email from the prospective group and this dance would continue until the potential new international affiliate gave up hope and looked elsewhere. I was impotent to manage international affiliate development and seemingly powerless to coordinate my own.

Stewart was great. When he had decided to join he had rung, an unexpected call one Thursday morning. After a short flurry of questions he said he was interested and asked what I was up to on Saturday – I would be at home, it was the middle of *Kangeiko* as we had started the Japanese tradition ourselves once we had opened the full-time dojo. Great, came the reply, I'll fly over. Two days later he and three of the JKA Scotland seniors flew in to Dublin and we spent a pleasant day talking things over, finding common ground and making a plan. He was intelligent and shrewd. He also seemed to be hard-working, almost a workaholic. Holding down a sales job for a local manufacturing company, he also ran a full-time dojo in Dunfermline with over 500 students. If that wasn't enough, he was also the head of the group, boasting fifty dojos and 2,000 members. The JKS GB & Ireland had just doubled in size and he was someone I could definitely work with.

The following month I flew over to teach one Tuesday evening. Stewart seemed to be doing very few sales, apart from the occasional quick-fire phone call to clients that I struggled to understand. I was shown his dojo and several other professional dojos in the area that all belonged to the group. After a pleasant day of tea, cake and conversation, we made our way back to his dojo and I taught a packed room of black belts. They were good. A little rigid, which often characterizes JKA karate outside Japan, but they were keen and talented. I was happy to teach, then drink pints and eat Chinese – these were my type of people! They instantly became active members of the group and despite the constant criticism from Japan, I enjoyed working with them. I became a regular visitor to the JKS Scotland headquarters and enjoyed their company. They were often harsh and dominating – very Celtic – but I loved their company and I think at times they forgave me my Englishness. Strangely, Peter never really ingratiated himself with them. Shortly after I visited midweek to teach, Peter did the same. We were both paid well to teach an excited group of young dynamic black belts for ninety minutes. It was a dream gig, but apparently Peter had been grumpy and less than friendly. Over the next year I urged Stewart to try several more times with Peter, but with whatever was between them, they failed to connect.

Several months later we arranged a JKS Scotland technical seminar with a Headquarters instructor and myself. They sent Hirota, who did a splendid job showing exactly what the young, dynamite instructors from Japan could do. After the seminar Hirota furtively arranged to have a meeting with Stewart and the seniors. They bundled themselves into a room and Hirota used a Japanese member of Stewart's dojo to translate the request. I was informed that my *kohai* had insisted I didn't attend, so I sat outside, like someone stood up for an important date. It had Takahashi Sempai written all over it. Part of me was outraged. How could they treat me like this? After everything I had done to build the JKS in the British Isles and farther afield. At the same time, what else had I expected? Would they have handled things in any other way? My Western side screamed injustice. My Eastern side simply shrugged and muttered, '*Shou ga nai.*'

Apparently, the meeting was successful. The JKS accepted Stewart's membership. I was unsure what a twenty-minute meeting, translated by a guy who lacked real competency in English, could achieve that I hadn't already, but we all knew that wasn't really the point. However, Stewart had my trust and I his. He had been under great pressure from the JKA, treated appallingly and let down by them on several occasions. He had the measure of Japanese-based organizations and was well beyond putting them on a pedestal. When he left the JKA, and in order to bring his whole group with him he had had to make promises and commitments to his members that were not concurrent with the way JKS ran things. I turned a blind eye and Peter never knew. He was in a bind and his actions had the best of motivations. Although I slowly felt the hand of Japan dishonourably trying to swoop up all my hard work, I was confident in my relationship with all the JKS GB & Ireland members. This was my community, which I had built up. I was secure in the position I had created.

In autumn 2008, after a certain amount of lobbying,

we were given the job of hosting the first JKS European Championships. Despite the attempts of certain instructors within the Headquarters to cull my perceived powers, my group had grown steadily over the last six years. The JKS GB & Ireland was the natural choice to host the inaugural tournament. It was decided that Cambridge would be a suitable and convenient location for international teams and a three-day technical seminar and competition was arranged. Sueki was given the job of leading the technical seminar, ably assisted by our sempai, Koyama, and myself. Sueki arrived, jet-lagged, on Thursday evening and went straight to bed. Koyama Sempai arrived early Friday morning, ready for the evening's start. We arranged to meet for lunch at a Wagamama restaurant close to the sports centre and halfway through our mains Sueki announced he had a message from Takahashi Sempai.

'Scott, on the information for the course and championships you wrote you had graduated from the Instructors' Course. This is not correct.'

'Yeah, I know,' I said, stuffing a gyoza into my mouth. 'The problem is that no one really understands the difference between *Kenshusei* and *Shugyosei*. So I just translate it to "Instructors' Course".' (*Kenshusei* derives from three words: *Ken* – to polish, *Shu* – mastery and *Sei* – person. *Shugyosei* came from two, *Shugyo* – martial/spiritual training at the highest level and *Sei* – person. 'Instructors' Course' was shorthand for both.)

'No.' Sueki, stopped, as if readying himself. 'You never graduated.'

I looked at Koyama Sempai. He looked back at me, equally puzzled, confirming I hadn't misunderstood Sueki's Japanese.

'What?'

'You never graduated. You have to stop telling people you graduated, this is a lie.' He looked down at his miso soup, unable to meet my glare. I felt sick with anger and stood up.

'You were there, Sueki – at my graduation!' I spat out the words in my most guttural Japanese. He was like my brother, and yet again he had been sent to do Takahashi Sempai's dirty work. I stormed out of Wagamama. The restaurant's name translates as 'selfish' – how apt. Takahashi Sempai was rapidly changing the rules and history of the JKS for his own goals. I found it hard to even meet Sueki's gaze over the next few days. But just as before I eventually forgave him, knowing that he was merely doing what he had to do. I no longer lived in that strict regime of *osues* and bows, but he did.

Koyama Sempai found me later. 'What do you think?' I asked him.

'You graduated,' he said, with a shrug of his shoulders. That's all he could say – what else was there? We all knew what the issue was.

But I just couldn't let it go. Later I questioned the Headquarters. I had to send them a copy of my certificate and eventually Yumoto Sensei, knowing the truth, fudged the issue, saying I had completed the course, but not graduated – it was ridiculous, but I was past caring by that stage, and let it slide. I wish I had known then that years later it would come back to bite me in the arse.

The championships were a huge success, but throughout the event I had that familiar sinking feeling. This would continue to resurface every time I had to deal with Japan. As the year drew to a close, the JKS GB & Ireland, my dojo and my career were everything I could have dreamt of. All our cooperative hard work had paid off and I derived great joy from my karate. In my personal life, Tor and I had our daughter in the spring of 2008 and were deliriously happy, a happiness darkly mirrored by my dealings with Japan.

For example, it became a running joke that two or three weeks before any major seminar I would receive a phone call in the middle of the night from Takahashi Sempai. He would always demand things I couldn't deliver. From wanting to change flights, change instructors, change training times, change fees paid; or forbidding me from holding examinations, preventing me from teaching in various countries or simply trying to elevate anyone around me to undermine the power he thought I had. It was relentless. Then and now, it seems petty and insecure that I would care, but every time I visited Japan it was always commented on that I had become fat. Often flanked by Peter and Stewart, who were undeniably more portly than me, I would be targeted for ridicule whilst the others were exempt. I knew it was puerile and I tried to ignore the constant criticism whilst denying them the reaction they sought, but it spoke to a much deeper animosity that was developing.

On one course I taught a black-belt class as Takahashi Sempai lurked at the back. I created a few interesting ways to maximize and highlight the snap of one's shoulders when executing blocks, punches or strikes. According to those in attendance, it was well thought-out, helpful and really dealt with the problem so many western karate-*ka* experience, the over-reliance on stiff, upper bodies. On this particular course both Takahashi Sempai and Yamada Sempai were the main instructors. During the break we drank water and prepared our next class. Yamada Sempai had the same group as I had taught. Ignoring me, he asked Takahashi Sempai what I had done with the class. 'Just blocks,' came the dismissive reply. It summed up the whole dynamic. I laboured and slogged away to create a good class, a good dojo, a good organization. In response my sempai ignored my efforts, favoured others and found ways to undermine my position.

On the same course, Takahashi Sempai ordered me to change the name of my dojo. How arrogant, he said, that I would call my school the Hombu Dojo (headquarters), as if I represented the JKS in any way. I had christened my dojo six years earlier. On initial visits he had commented on how much he liked my logo and had gladly received Hombu Dojo-branded merchandise: a rucksack, a T-shirt, a towel and a sweater. Now I had to completely rebrand. I simply said '*osu*', knowing I would never do such a thing. It was a far cry from six years ago.

The Japanese often talk about one's personal stock; what people think of you. When in Japan, through the investment of hard work and sweat, I'd gained a lot of 'stock'. I left the Instructors' Course with an abundance of goodwill and as a result my market value back home had such a boost with what I had achieved in Japan. But it seemed that the more I invested my stock in the European market, the more my Japanese investment ebbed away. As my popularity increased in the West, my relationship with the East was reaching a point of no return. The only saving grace was that all animosity seemed to emanate from Takahashi Sempai. Shortly after the issue about the renaming of my dojo I spoke to Yumoto Sensei. I mentioned if it was okay to call my dojo Hombu; after all, even in Japan each region has its own Hombu, let alone international affiliates.

'Yes, of course,' came the response. 'Why?'

'Well, Takahashi Sempai told me I couldn't use the name.'

'Ah,' he said with a certain recognition in his voice. 'Don't worry about it.' That was enough for me to fret no more. But

I knew that Yumoto Sensei wouldn't deal with this dispute. On this occasion I would be allowed to win by stealth, but the main problem wasn't dealt with head on and as a result all these matters were allowed to fester and develop. I still had a great many friends in Japan, but it was an unavoidable truth that sooner or later these issues would have to be resolved. And I didn't expect it to end well.

SEVEN

From an early age I wanted to do karate for a living. I had once read an interview with Frank Brennan Sensei in Terry O'Neil's *Fighting Arts International*. He mentioned that he had never really had a job, briefly working in a shop, before becoming a full-time instructor. I had also heard that he'd even been offered a place on the Instructors' Course by Nakayama Sensei, but turned it down because his career had been going so well. I instantly felt jealous of him – how could I not have to have a job? Of course, the answer was, by working exceptionally hard.

My band of friends, helping to push each other on at morning training, Dublin, July 2008.

When I was young I trained extremely hard. I then went to university and trained even harder. After graduating I moved to Japan and found out what real hard training was. Not content, I then entered the Instructors' Course and trained to a level that few can even imagine. This was my investment, my preparation for the future. I was determined to be like Frank Brennan and never have to have a normal job. Plus, when I was young, Ishii Sensei had told me that people must train hard until they are thirty and then their training will last a lifetime.

But after a few years in Ireland and a few years after my thirtieth birthday, I realized that the investment I had made in Japan had to be constantly topped up. I also realized that Ishii Sensei had lied to me. He may have got away with it, but I couldn't. Of course, Gayle and I had always done our personal training, which had been tough, but as time went on more had joined our morning group. With the opening of our full-time dojo, we had our own home and could train whenever we wanted. A schedule developed organically and we soon found ourselves training Tuesday, Wednesday and Thursday mornings. Members changed their work schedules, insisted on flexi-time and lied about fake meetings in order to be part of the morning crew. With a regular group of twelve, some training every day, others just once a week, we had created the perfect environment to develop and evolve together. I never taught, just led. With all the equipment we needed, training advanced and progressed as I stole ideas from friends, colleagues and Facebook. Ankle weights took the role of *Tetsu-Geta*[1] and Thera-bands more than adequately replaced bicycle inner tubes for tube training. It was tough, hard training interspersed with friendly banter

1. *Tetsu-Geta* – iron shoes used to strengthen legs.

and self-deprecating humour. To be honest it was mainly me taking the piss whilst my friends graciously took it: they were, and still are, very kind to humour me.

Occasionally we would have a visitor, maybe an instructor or a regular dojo member who wanted to step up to the big league. As always with a close-knit group, without saying a word everyone upped their game. Rest periods were shortened and morning crew members popped out techniques whilst the newbies struggled to keep up. Some came once, never to be seen again, others struggled on, persevered and became part of the group. The most important thing was that it was like Instructors' Training at the Headquarters, but accessible for everyone.

Harry was a medical doctor in his mid-fifties. A fit and energetic guy, he trained religiously every morning. He had a great knowledge of *kata* and was always the go-to guy when it came to small details of Shotokan and non-Shotokan forms. In Japan, when a question was raised, Yumoto Sensei always sent Sueki to the office to check Nakayama Sensei's *Best Karate*; in my dojo, we just asked Harry.

Richard was a vet from Hungary. When he first came to my dojo I caught him lurking outside and startled him by asking him if I could help.

'I would like some information about karate,' he requested.

'Ah, I think you may have come to the right place,' was the sort of humour that went straight over his head. I tried the more direct approach. 'Here is a beginners' pack.'

'I am not a beginner,' he said with a smidgeon of arrogance. We soon became good friends. He lived near Fergus's dojo, but would stay well clear of it and make the 45 km round trip in rush hour traffic every morning to attend my training. He was young, dynamic and with a background of sports karate, and he moved well, if not biomechanically correctly.

Thomas was a different kettle of fish. A Romanian black belt, he had begun training with me long before I opened the Hombu. I remember the first time he walked into the Iveagh Centre one Wednesday night. He had been training with the JKA but was looking for something different. He trained well and afterwards found me in the changing rooms.

'Scott, great class, can I pay please?' he said, handing over the money as I was drying myself after my shower.

'Thomas, I never take money from men when I'm naked,' I said, letting the stupid part of my brain take control as the rest of my thought-processing self screamed about the inappropriate nature of saying something like that to a potential student. Thankfully, he laughed. He was funny, laid back and would often come to morning training, occasionally training hard, but mostly laughing at how the rest of us we were practically killing ourselves for the art.

On one occasion we had introduced a particularly hard training regime to the end of our normal set. Involving difficult press-ups, crunches and planks, we set about the 15-minute ordeal. Halfway through I heard, 'Ah, fuck this!' and saw Thomas heading for the showers, perfectly verbalizing what everyone else was thinking. But only he could get away with it. He was talented, sharp and knowledgeable, successfully progressing through the grades over the years. In fact all of them, through hard work and dedication, successfully graded with Yumoto Sensei and Takahashi Sempai, becoming senior members of the JKS GB & Ireland. I was proud of them professionally and thankful for their friendship.

What my merry band of hard trainers allowed me to do was have dedicated time to my own karate. I was desperate to keep my edge and not become irrelevant in the art I had decided to dedicate my life to. Feeling their expectancy of a tough session, I was obliged to train three times a week and when there, train hard. Through the constant repetition of the same training menu, I was able to see and feel the nuances of what I was doing. In Japan, fear and exhaustion had blocked such subtleties, but with the weight of my sempai lifted from my shoulders, I was free to allow my subconscious to investigate the minutiae of what we were experiencing. This often led to new insights, which I constantly translated to ideas for weekend seminars. I often feared that my classes were all the same: hips, hips and more hips. But in essence using one's hips correctly was the foundation of everything we did. So I persevered and tried to conjure up more and more interesting ways of teaching correct form and posture; trying to take inspiration from visiting Japanese instructors whilst pushing myself harder.

On one particular spring technical seminar Yumoto Sensei kicked off with his normal muscle-training class. This time he introduced a series of squatting exercises that lasted three minutes. Professional pride made me see out the drill, but as I stood up the relief in my legs spread upwards and I think my body couldn't figure out if I was experiencing intense pain or orgasmic pleasure! I looked around. The dojo was full of exhausted black belts, and we were thirty minutes into a three-day, ten-hour technical seminar. Yumoto Sensei then went on to tell us that in Instructors' Training they did three sets of three minutes with only a one-minute break in between. Participants looked on with awe at this superhuman athlete, but over the next day few could move well as the lactic acid took its toll and limited their ability to get the most from the seminar. Peter complained to me and I am sure his views were shared by many; in fact, one dojo that had recently joined left shortly after.

Later that evening, as we sat in the restaurant, Yumoto spoke. 'Scott, do you know I have been made JKS Chief Instructor?'

'No, Sensei. When was this?' I was genuinely surprised. The last I had heard, Taguchi Sensei would forever be Chief Instructor. Maybe I had misunderstood the announcement after his funeral.

'Last week.' I congratulated him. 'Does anyone know? Maybe you should make an announcement.' I was just about to get everyone's attention when he leant over and asked: 'Wait, is everyone here?'

'No Sensei, we are still waiting for the Swedish and German group.'

'Okay,' he said. 'Let's wait until they arrive.'

Thirty minutes and several glasses of wine later, it had slipped my mind.

'Scott, is everyone here now?'

'Yes, Sensei.'

'Okay, make the announcement.'

I stood up, as if making a best man's speech. 'Guys, I have an announcement. Yumoto Sensei has recently been made JKS Chief Instructor!' There was an instant round of applause and congratulations from the twenty or so European seniors. Yumoto Sensei looked surprised.

'No, no,' he said, gesturing for them to calm down. 'It's nothing …' His theatrical modesty didn't work, and they continued to toast his promotion whilst he looked on, pretending to be embarrassed. It was ego. Yumoto Sensei was one of the most talented karate-*ka* in the world, dedicated and inspiring, but we all have an ego.

The following week I received an email from the

Headquarters. Apparently I had underpaid him. His *per diem* had increased due to his promotion and I now owed him a further $500. I hadn't been informed, however, and it was always our practice to give him a bonus. I did the maths, and when the extra was included and currency conversation had been taken into account, he had received his new salary. But why couldn't he have just spoken to me face to face? The

Teaching in Norway, July 2010. From left to right: Aidan Trimble 7th dan, Steve Ubl 8th dan, Tom Kompier 6th dan, Richard Amos 7th dan and myself.

Japanese have perfected the dichotomy of *Honne* (true feelings) and *Tatemae* (façade). In Japan anything public can be seen as false and unauthentic. Developed over centuries as a response to the crushing social norms and feudal hierarchy, it is now the perfect system to cope with the modern, overcrowded metropolises of the archipelago. I just didn't expect it with Yumoto Sensei. He was an honest and forthright man, but almost paradoxically to his profession, I don't think he liked confrontation. After his superhuman squats performance during the seminar, the theatre over dinner and the farce with his salary, my view of my sensei was given a reality check.

I returned to my dojo with very little inspiration to help move the group forward during the next three months of upcoming courses, but we did decide to see if we could build up to the three sets of three-minute killer squats. It took us four weeks, or twelve sessions of morning training, to build up to the level. From Harry, the mild-mannered doctor in his fifties, down to members of the morning crew in their twenties, we were all successful. Yumoto Sensei had a point: we do need such exercises to increase physical ability, so the lessons we learn in classes and seminars can be put into practice. However, everyone on the recent spring seminar left with the impression that the level set was impossible to attain – it wasn't, and so I set about trying to dispel the superhuman impression that professional, full-time instructors like to portray. It was our job to be fit, fast and sharp. It was then our job to help and inspire our students to fulfil their potential in whatever way possible.

Later on in the year I had the opportunity to train with Steve Ubl Sensei. Koyama Sempai had often spoken about him and I knew that Richard Sempai in the States had started working with him. Steve Sensei had been made Technical Director of Richard Sempai's group, the WTKO. I had been told both Richard Sempai and Steve Sensei were teaching in the UK late in November. I had nothing scheduled, so on a rare free weekend I decided to travel over. Peter hesitated and then finally decided not to come along, but a number of the senior members of the JKS in England supported the camp and we attended a packed two-day event. It was great to see Richard Sempai again. We had kept in touch and in fact had taught with each other every year on the Norwegian Shotokan Federation's summer camp, a group that was still affiliated to both the WTKO and JKS.

I was excited to meet Steve Sensei. Koyama Sempai had filled me in. He was the first student of Nakayama Sensei's Hoitsugan Dojo, the JKA Chief Instructor's private dojo. Steve Sensei had moved to Japan in 1972 to train at the JKA Headquarters. Shortly after, Nakayama Sensei had come to him and asked where he was staying. When he heard of his cheap student accommodation, Nakayama Sensei told him to collect his stuff and bring it to the Headquarters the next day. Steve Sensei arrived at the allotted time and Nakayama Sensei led him to his new house: first floor dojo, second floor dormitory, third floor of the Nakayama family home. This was the start of a close ten-year friendship with Nakayama Sensei during the height of JKA fame. Steve Sensei travelled backwards and forwards to Japan over the years and whilst back home completed Nishiyama Sensei's Instructors' Course, which was considered equal to the one in Japan. In 1984 for political and personal reasons, Steve Sensei withdrew from the mainstream karate community and trained by himself and with a select few, refining and developing the lessons he had learnt in Japan. When Richard Sempai met him he still maintained the rank of 2nd dan, which he had received from Nakayama Sensei. Richard Sempai had immediately invited him into the WTKO, asked him to be Technical Director and the Executive Committee had awarded him 7th dan. This was so unusual that I was desperate to see what all the fuss was about.

Oh my God! My view of karate was immediately

revolutionized. In many ways it was the perfect antidote to Yumoto Sensei's course. I hadn't been searching for anything and didn't need a new direction. I knew there weren't any hidden secrets. Karate worked and I knew that the only way to success was through hard training, but what Steve Sensei taught had such depth that I was blown away.

The following weekend Peter was in Ireland. It had now become tradition that he would teach for me on the JKS Ireland Christmas Course and I would go over the following week to jointly teach with him on the JKS GB Christmas Course. Over dinner one evening, disappointed that he had decided not to train with Steve Sensei, I tried to describe what I had experienced.

Peter wasn't particularly enthusiastic. 'So what exactly did he teach?'

'Well, maybe you and I teach the technique and maybe the in-between bit of the techniques. But Steve Sensei teaches the in-between bits of the in-between bits.' I don't think he quite got what I was trying to say.

'Well if he's that bloody good, why don't we leave the JKS and join them?' he retorted, slightly agitated. I quickly changed the subject.

To be fair to Peter, when I was on the course there must have been nearly a hundred black belts crowded into the packed dojo. At one point I looked around and most of them seemed to be scratching their heads, at a loss to what Steve Sensei was trying to teach – understandably, as it was a far cry from what I, and I presume they, had ever experienced. I still gleaned as much information as possible and along with quite a few fresh ideas I stole from Richard Sempai, I left the course invigorated and with enough 'material' to last me a year.

The decade drew to an end, and I felt that the last ten years had been well spent. Two years on the Instructors' Course followed by eight years building a dojo and a strong group had really paid off. I had 500 members in the dojo and had recently taken on a third full-time instructor, who happened to be Koyama Sempai. He had left France several years earlier and not wanting to return to Japan, had worked a little in Italy and then travelled the world, like a warrior monk, teaching his awesome style of karate. But by 2010 he was ready to settle down again and I eagerly offered him a job. It was as if a little Irish genie had popped out of a bottle of Guinness and said, 'Right, Scott, tell me what you really want.' and had then gone on to create a perfect dream situation. Ireland had been incredibly kind to me and Koyama Sempai arrived at just the right moment. For the last year or so my physio Michael Thompson, who just happened to be former European Kyokushin Karate Champion and Japanese K1 Fighter, had been insisting that I reduce my schedule.

'Scott,' he said in true sempai fashion, 'either you reduce the amount of hours you teach in the dojo or you reduce the amount of weekends away you teach. If you don't, something will break and you will destroy your career.' He would then point to his massage table and say, 'Get over there, I'm going to go medieval on your arse!' I would scream and cry as he sought to rectify my self-abuse through overwork. 'Pain is just weakness leaving the body,' he would insist, as only he could.

I took his advice and reduced my teaching schedule to just two days a week. Koyama Sempai taught three days and then was also away most weekends teaching seminars. I continued to teach weekend seminars, but had hit saturation point of forty per year and could cherry-pick the good ones. The group had also grown to over a hundred dojos and we were now one of the biggest single-style groups in the British Isles. What was more important was that we were growing whilst all other groups continued to implode. Life was good.

Certain relationships suffered. The year before Koyama Sempai came to work for me, Fergus had decided to leave the dojo. His success at the World Championships in 2007 had been followed by similar success in the Europeans in 2008. As positive as that was, issues started to arise back in the dojo. I had made him squad coach. He was still heavily involved in competition, and I felt he was best able to take the squad forward. However, I started to receive complaints. These were reinforced by the fact that he was haemorrhaging students in the classes he taught for me. It is the nature of the business to get complaints and receive criticism, especially when you have 500+ students, but when I had to act as employer to employee, Fergus took it personally. He had taken 5th dan and was now the same grade as me. Somewhere deep in his psyche I believed he wondered why I was getting all the prestigious weekend seminars whilst he was sidelined to teach white-belt kids in the suburbs. I think the success of the dojo looked easy and the success of my international career was perceived to have been bestowed on me by my position as JKS GB & Ireland Technical Director. Like many in the group, he had joined a successful organization. Many, I am sure, believed my group was successful because it was affiliated to the JKS, but if they had bothered to look at JKS-affiliated groups in other countries, they would have understood the inaccuracy of their theory.

When my daughter arrived unexpectedly almost a month early in April 2008, Tor and I suddenly found ourselves premature parents. I texted Fergus and my other full-time instructor to see if they could cover my classes for a fortnight

– although we had discussed it, no schedule had been finalized. I later heard that Fergus had insisted that he teach all adult classes, implying my other instructor was too junior to teach anything other than kids' classes – he was a 4th dan with over twenty-five years of experience. Shortly afterwards, I mentioned that I was investigating the possibility of inviting Koyama Sempai to teach at the Hombu Dojo full time. 'Well, Scott, before you do that, what I need from you is at least two or three more classes a week,' he demanded rather naively.

'I'm sorry, Fergus. My responsibilities are to the dojo and the JKS GB & Ireland. If we get a chance to have another Instructors' Course graduate here, then I have to take it.' I had offered him part-time work, which helped me expand and helped him quit taxi-driving. I didn't owe him anymore, especially when I was constantly having to 're-stock' his existing classes. But the final straw came when on a JKS Ireland technical seminar, Fergus put forward five of his own dojo students to take 1st dan. The visiting 7th dan instructor wanted to fail them all, they were that poor. Peter and I convinced the examiner to at least pass one, which he did, reluctantly. Fergus was furious. He claimed to one of the seniors that this was all political and believed I was responsible for them failing, then stormed out of the dojo.

The following morning he sent me an email informing me he wished to quit teaching at the Hombu Dojo and would give me two weeks' notice. I rang him.

'Are you sure?' I asked, knowing that his knee-jerk reaction forbade him from changing his mind. 'What will you do?' We were at the height of the worst financial crisis ever to hit Ireland.

'Yes, I'm sure. I'll go back to taxiing.' I knew that in the last few years everyone who had lost their jobs or were on reduced hours had turned to taxiing and delivery work. Tor and I had had pizza delivered by a man in a three-piece suit driving a Bentley! Things were tough out there.

JKS Ireland Squad at the JKS World Championships in Edinburgh, September 2011.

'Okay,' I said, 'then you stop immediately'. I didn't want a disgruntled employee teaching in the dojo for two weeks. Besides, one of my part-time instructors had bitten my hand off when I had offered her four more classes per week – she had suddenly become a full-time karate instructor, earning a liveable wage on nine hours per week; it was good money. Fergus would continue to act as squad coach, but our relationship deteriorated significantly. Peter and Stewart advised me to just expel him from the group, as every time I had any dealing with him there was always a quarrel or disagreement. He would still occasionally show up for morning training because, as they say in Ireland, he was bold and no one would tell him to cop on. Predictably it would make for an atmosphere in the dojo and as soon as he stopped training regularly he struggled to keep up, especially as our training was always evolving. The differences made it difficult for him to excel as he once had done.

When Koyama Sempai arrived in Ireland I had the opportunity to reduce Fergus's role to Kata coach, making Koyama Sempai Kumite coach. This was a further nail in the coffin of our relationship. Fergus wasn't a competition fighter – he was a great technician. Koyama Sempai was a former All-Japan Kumite Champion, former captain of Teikyo University and graduate of the Instructors' Course. But Fergus felt that the squad should be coached by an Irish karate-*ka*. I pointed out that the Irish soccer team was coached by an Italian, but his lack of logic forbade him from seeing my point. He was a monument to belligerence, a pariah of peevishness, a catalyst for confrontation – in short, he was a pain in the arse.

But the truth is that there is never one truth. I genuinely liked the chap. He was funny, charismatic and talented. He deserved to be in a position of power within the group. Fergus had all the skills to play a vital role, but we all live in a spectrum. Often an individual can work hard, collaborate and toil as he or she moves up the ladder of their chosen pursuit. The difficulty is not achieving one's goals; the difficulty is in maintaining the skills that got you there in the first place.

Years ago I formulated my theory of karate group dynamics. No one starts karate because it is enjoyable – if you want fun, play a team sport. People come to karate seeking something: maybe for self-defence, maybe because they feel weak, timid, or shy. They want to be faster, stronger, more self-confident. Either way, it is often an insecurity that drives that desire to do karate. The bigger the insecurity, the harder they train.

The harder they train, the better they become. The better they become the higher the rank they achieve. The higher the rank they achieve the bigger chance they have of gaining a position of power. And the more power they gain the more insecure they become. It's a terrible negative feedback loop. In many ways the drive that got Fergus to where he was, was so strong it meant he was incapable of the cooperation and compromise that is vital in such a role.

His opinion was entirely different, of course. I was a controlling, manipulative and dictatorial head of the group. I am sure he had a point. *I'm not bossy, it's just that I have better ideas* is a sign one of my instructors recently gave me. But I always tried to seek consensus. Tor has always been a sounding board for all issues within the group. She has a naturally ability, like any good partner, to disagree with every point of view I have. I really had to justify decisions to her and, therefore myself. Despite Peter and Stewart calling for his blood, especially when his pugnaciousness spilt over to international events, I listened to Tor and tried to find a way for him.

The last straw finally came at the 2011 World Championships, which Stewart was hosting in Scotland. There had been further changes with the squad. Koyama Sempai had unfortunately decided to move back to France. He had been offered a great job in the country he loved, so, understandably, took it. I used the job vacancy to bring some new energy into the group. I head-hunted. Palma Diosi from Hungary, where she had been twenty times National All-Styles Champion. She took on the role of *kumite* coach, bringing a host of new ideas. An enlarged Irish squad travelled to Edinburgh via coach to compete in the biggest event the JKS had ever seen. Fergus refused to use the financially viable mode of transport and flew instead. Now that Koyama Sempai was out of the picture, he tried to dictate like never before, bossing Palma about in true misogynistic fashion. Palma took it in her stride – with over thirty years' experience, she was more than used to the male karate ego. But when Fergus's son lost in the first round of his *kumite* event, his reaction was immediately transmitted to me by several onlookers. He was enraged by his child's defeat and reacted in a way that was emotionally charged. Onlookers just saw a big guy with 'Irish Team Squad Coach' on his jacket dealing dominantly with a team member. Hours later he was on the mat himself, winning the Veterans' Kata title again. Unlike four years ago, when humility had been the order of the day, he now paraded himself like never before, wearing his medal around his neck like a gong of reflected glory. My irritation reached fever point and after the incident with his son there was no return. I spoke to him, but he denied that anything had happened. He dismissed the onlookers as fantasists. However, there was no grand conspiracy. I had no choice, I removed him as squad coach and although he remained in the JKS, we hardly spoke again.

Although I saw the deterioration of my relationship with Fergus and my inability to help him reach his potential as a professional failure, I never felt the personal loss. Peter, on the other hand, had been my friend and sempai for close to a quarter of a century. I had modelled my dojo and my initial career on him. When we first joined forces he was thirty-nine years old and had spent that decade working hard to build a solid dojo with seven locations and 150 members. But before long his dojo had dropped to seventy members and he was becoming reliant on the occasional gigs he got from the JKS. Within a few years Simon had given up attending his dojo, as every time Peter got wind that Simon was on the way, he just wouldn't turn up, leaving the class to the commuting senior. I had heard similar stories from others. Most of his younger students had left. Attrition is part and parcel of any dojo, but for the majority of his young guns to leave was difficult to understand.

As early as 2006 I had to have a very difficult but necessary conversation with him about his business model. I sat him down one Saturday night when we shared an apartment in Stavanger, Norway. I pointed out that his dojo was his bread and butter. If the prestige and excitement of being invited to weekend gigs suddenly disappeared, then we must make a sustainable living from our dojos. Seventy members just wasn't enough; he needed to focus on his own guys as well. He took it well and said he appreciated the mini intervention.

'I understand.' He sipped his wine. 'Jesus, I feel like I've been on *The Apprentice*. Besides, I'll never get much weekend work … not like you,' he concluded, rather bitterly.

But brief moments of clarity weren't enough. His dojo never truly recovered and it seemed that he was increasingly reliant on the JKS as a revenue source. It started as a trickle, but before long there was a steady stream of issues that seniors in England were making me aware of. It started with one dojo thirty minutes' drive from Peter's house being charged £50 for travel expenses. Peter had implemented a fixed cost-per-mile expense, taking into account the devaluation of his car, rather than just the cost of petrol used. As far as I knew, this type of thing only existed in the corporate world. I really didn't have the authority to intervene in what he charged for travel, but I knew he was prohibiting repeat business. Then his fees started to increase. For a long time we had taken our lead from the Headquarters. Instructors our grade charged €250 per day. Peter started to charge £250 and then before long it was £300. Clubs would often look at my fees and even with a Ryanair flight, the total expense for a course with me was less than Peter's daily fee alone. Furthermore, as my 'stock' increased, my seminars attracted participants from farther afield than the host dojo. I was becoming increasingly popular and Peter was losing out.

When courses were less than forthcoming, Peter started to encourage people to come to him. He had always conducted black- and brown-belt seminars, maybe eight per year. But it was pointed out to me that he had started insisting that all JKS brown belts must attend if they wish to grade for black belt, which translated to all brown belts in the group. He then tried to implement a rule that all 1st Kyu grading must take place on these seminars. What had started as special voluntary black- and brown-belt seminars for his dojo had morphed into compulsory, national, high-grade seminars. I had to have a serious conversation with him on behalf of the dojo heads who dared only complain to me. It slowly ate away at our friendship and I am sure he felt I was limiting his ability to earn a living, which was in high contrast to what I was doing. In the first year of him joining the JKS, we earned about the same salary. I now feared there was a huge difference in our income. I knew his approach of compulsory courses and high teaching fees was a recipe for disaster. If only he would concur.

By the end of the decade, due to increased international work, I only visited English clubs a few times a year, so chances to influence my friend were limited and often fell on deaf ears. The highlight of the year was the JKS England Christmas Course. I would turn up and find maybe twenty or thirty participants in the venue, most of whom were dojo heads and students from other JKS-affiliated clubs. Peter seemed unconcerned with attendance. We would share profits and he was under no pressure to pay me my daily rate. The black- and brown-belt training that he would consistently hold two weeks prior to our course always had double or triple the attendees of our 'open to all grades' course. Similarly, the following week his dojo held the end-of-year kyu grading, where everyone was far more motivated to attend. I convinced myself I didn't care. I rarely made my daily fee at that time, but very quickly found myself booked for the Sunday and Monday following the Christmas course. These other gigs became regular, lucrative events and I was happy just to see all the JKS England seniors together once a year.

Around the same time he seemed to become far less willing to compromise with what I needed. He continued his tradition of coming to Ireland every December to teach and help out with my Christmas course and grading. This was the last in the three annual national seminars with visiting international instructors that I had committed to all that time ago. With often in excess of 300 people in attendance, I gave Peter a door split and it was very profitable. One year I was eager to invite Kitagawa Sensei, who was a senior instructor based in the US. He couldn't attend any other time than the December course so I rang Peter to explain the situation.

'I wanted Kitagawa Sensei to come to the March course, but he can't make it. Are you free then?' Kitagawa Sensei would be a huge boost for the group and I hoped I could work it out. 'Great. You're free. So can you do that one?'

'Is that as well as or instead of the Christmas course?' he asked. 'Oh, instead of … which is busier?'

'Well, the Christmas course is always the busiest,' I said,

not really wondering why he was asking.

'Well in that case I will leave it as it is,' he said, as if it were his choice.

On the Sunday evening of the Christmas course as we left my house and made our way to the dojo's Christmas party, I handed him a thick brown envelope stuffed with more cash than I had ever given anyone. With a thankful 'Oh, cheers' he stuffed it into his coat pocket. When we arrived he made his way to the toilet. Ten minutes later, as I met and greeted students I found the same envelope, empty and screwed up on a table next to the loos. He had obviously been keen to see how much he had been paid. The abandoned stationery seemed to speak volumes.

Around that time he asked me to organize a trip to Japan over the Easter period. He had university students who could only go during the break. Despite Tor's protest, I did as requested and put together the annual trip, taking in the Headquarters, Yokose Sensei's dojo and Hokkaido. Information was sent out and a date for payment of flights was set up three months hence. As the time drew closer I had many confirmations and it was turning out to be one of the most popular trips I had done in a long time – it would be a lot of hard work. But the date for the initial payment came and went and I never received anything from Peter and his three students. I called him.

'Oh yeah, they can't go,' Peter informed me, as if it had slipped his mind.

'But I'm organizing the trip for your guys!' I found it hard to suppress my anger and frustration.

'Well, I can't force them to go.'

'Yeah, but *you* can come. It's a big group, all from England, and no one has been before. It's very stressful. I need help,' I pleaded.

There was a pregnant pause. 'I'd rather not,' he finally said, allowing my pleas to fall on deaf ears. So the Monday before Easter I left my sad daughter and disgruntled wife for the entire holiday and took eighteen members of JKS England to Japan. They, of course, had a great time. However, by that point I felt I was public enemy number one at the Headquarters. I was a bundle of nerves for most of the trip, and all for Peter's sake. I knew then that as close as we were, as funny, warm and loving as my sempai could be, it was Peter v. Everyone Else. The steady stream of issues kept on flowing my way and by the end of the decade, scratch below the surface of our friendship and there was an ugly, festering, pus-filled abscess. But I understood. He never claimed to be anything else. I respected him and loved him as a big brother. The word love is bandied about with callous indifference, but my friendship with him wasn't blind. I understood his weaknesses, desires and drives, and still chose to be his friend. That was far better than labouring under a delusion. He was tough, strong, charismatic and a product of a harsh upbringing in Scotland. He had dragged himself up by the britches and made good. Like a survivor of a prisoner-of-war camp who still hoards food from the dinner table, the fact that he was highly functional was good enough to forgive him any of his idiosyncrasies. Besides, on this occasion, once I had got the visit to the Headquarters over and done with, the trip to Japan was a great success.

We made our way up to Hakkaido and spent a very pleasant few days in Sapporo. Sato Sensei was an 8th dan with the JKS and we had trained regularly together before I entered the Instructors' Course, as he had been based in Tokyo for a while. We landed at the regional airport to be greeted by the JKS-emblazoned senior. He bowed deeply to each member of the group, followed by the formal giving of his business card. But when he got to me all formalities disappeared and he gave me a hearty bear hug – most unexpected but greatly received. It helped remind me I still had friends in Japan.

Training was great, Sato Sensei was fantastic and at the end we had a large party with all his students. After he had presented each of my guys with the gift of a DVD containing a compilation of all Taguchi Sensei's *Koten* (ancient) *kata*, a resource that was like gold dust in the karate world, we set about being merry. One strange chap insisted on having an individual photograph with each member of my crew: it was only when he got to me that I realized he was insisting that we took the photo with our own cameras or phones. It was odd, but helped remind me why I loved Japan so much. Maybe I wasn't so pissed off with Peter as I initially thought.

My relationship with Stewart was very different. In many ways he was similar to Peter, although neither acknowledged such a thing and it appeared at times they barely put up with each other. After the initial few invites up to Scotland, Peter was no longer particularly welcome there and it was reciprocated by Stewart not being invited south of the border. But Stewart was busy and secure enough not to care. He ruled JKS Scotland with an iron fist and his guys seemed to give him loyalty of an unfathomable depth. He was successful and wealthy and I didn't begrudge him in the slightest, as he worked harder than anyone I knew. Being in his company was often hard but delightful. That brand of tough, cutting humour that Scottish people often use to show they care was sometime so close to the mark it hurt, but above all else he was solid, loyal and intelligent. I liked him and would speak to him a few times per week, but I never forgot what motivated him. He was a businessman.

Like Peter, he had an easily identifiable drive, albeit that their work ethics differed hugely. It was also to Stewart's credit that after many years of slowly increasing in girth he decided to do something about it. Many of us had lampooned and mocked him in the vague hope that he would get fit. However, he would dismiss the notion and call me a 'pussy' in his normal loving way, saying, as only someone could from the heart-disease capital of Europe could say, 'We are here for a good time, not a long time.' Then, in the spring of 2012, I think he took stock. The next time I saw him he was on the way to losing several stone, training every day, living on salad and had quit drinking. I was impressed by him: he was a great example for JKS Scotland, and they were lucky to have him.

Life meandered on. Taking stock in the autumn of 2012 I realized that nearly 100 per cent of my weekend courses were repeat business. I would turn up, from Birmingham to Bratislava, from Sri Lanka to Sweden, do a good job and my host would hand me an envelope with a 'thank you' and a 'see you next year'. My months were more synonymous with the countries I visited and far less with the unpredictable seasons of Ireland. May was always unseasonably warm, visiting Canada, USA and Germany; Novembers were always prematurely cold, visiting Norway, Denmark and Scotland. Every month took on its own personality, depending where I was.

The JKS GB & Ireland also reached its tenth birthday. We continued to grow, with big names like Matt Price – the former golden boy of the KUGB – joining, further legitimizing us and attracting more members. I still continued to invite instructors to teach at the three big grading seminars per year for my dojo, but as numbers had swelled, I added a second instructor on each course. The JKS in both the UK and Ireland was the envy of any group: regular courses with legitimate, high-profile instructors, annual trips to Japan, access to high-level international competitions and support for professional instructors. We were friendly, dedicated and we didn't rip people off. It wasn't rocket science.

However, I was struggling. The constant criticism and interference of Japan, the endless fire-fighting of Fergus created problems and the deterioration of my relationship with Peter was a relentless burden. In the September I mentioned to a senior instructor visiting from Birmingham that I was planning on taking a step back from the group in the next five years. Now a full-time instructor himself, he had nearly a quarter of a century of experience in the corporate world. 'Nonsense,' he said. 'When it comes down to it, you will never be able to walk away from what you have created.' Maybe he didn't realize how much pressure I was under. He was wrong. I knew my position within the JKS GB & Ireland was unsustainable and with everything I had done over the last decade – over the last three decades – it was always about what was sustainable, finding the third way.

Later on in the year Tor held a (not so) surprise fortieth birthday party for me. It was wonderful to see friends from all the facets of my life. Karate friends, university friends, family friends and friends I have no idea how I knew them were there. Fergus, of course, wasn't invited. Stewart had a plausible excuse. Peter just never came. Ten years ago, poor and just starting out, I had made a special effort to attend his surprise fortieth, and I remember him being delightfully shocked I was there. A decade later so much had changed. Happy to be around so many people I loved, I was sad how other parts of my life had evolved beyond my control. As I entered into my fifth decade I knew it was time for change.

EIGHT

2013 started off, like other recent years, with *Kangeiko*. No longer going to Japan for the event, the Hombu Dojo's version had gained a lot of momentum. We broke all records by having 113 members of the dojo and several international guests attend all or some of the week-long karate ordeal. I took great pride in knowing my *Kangeiko* was four times bigger than the one at the Headquarters. Furthermore, JKS Scotland had continued to grow too. Stewart, through his connection to the national governing body for karate, had made inroads bringing karate into schools. The group north of the border had swelled to 4,000 members. The JKS south of the boarder was doing equally well. Due to the shock revelation that Matt Price had left the KUGB, other clubs had followed suit. For the first time we had dojos in Wales. The expanded JKS England & Wales boasted forty dojos with over 2,000 members. In the last ten years the JKS GB & Ireland had grown to 120 dojos and over 8,000 members, and this was at a time when other, long-established groups were imploding.

Peter should have been happy, but in the decade he had been with us very few of the clubs had joined through him. Simon had been instrumental, travelling the country as he did, bringing the JKS brand to independent dojos. With my continued professional output, especially through social media, I too was contacted about affiliation. And now that

Matt Price was on board, he also became a major contributor to the group. Furthermore, I had become very good friends with Matt, Simon and Stewart. I felt it added to Peter's ill-ease. Matt was a mix of toughness and gentleness. Intelligent and talented, he was the fighter I never was. Stewart was shrewd, pragmatic and disciplined. He was the businessman I never was. Simon was simply the comedian I could never be. This didn't help Peter's sense of unease within the JKS GB & Ireland.

One evening that spring, over a few beers at the annual seminar with Yumoto Sensei, it came to a head and he erupted in frustration.

'What is the JKS GB & Ireland?' he demanded to know. 'I'm supposed to be chairman, but what does that even mean?' He was seriously pissed off.

'We have influence. We are leaders amongst equals and we guide the group.'

'What influence do I have in Scotland?'

And he was right. He had none. He had none in Ireland too. Apart from the annual trip to Dublin every Christmas, he was never invited. I knew he felt cheated out of the fruits of hard labour, but the fruits weren't of his hard labour. Stewart was frantic with his dojo, Matt and I were busy, teaching here, there and everywhere, and along with other seniors in the group, even Simon had started to get karate gigs, bringing his own special energy to the karate seminar scene. Peter, despite being the most senior member of the JKS GB & Ireland, was the least successful; his dojo was even small in comparison to others.

In Ireland my presence helped subdue any belligerence from Fergus, but when it was announced that the World Championships would be held in Japan in the summer, I had to deal with him once again. Due to his talent and skill he was a treasured member of the national team. He also had two able students who deserved a chance to compete at the highest level. He had, for most of the previous year, refused to attend Palma's squad sessions, holding his own instead, sometimes on the same day, at his dojo. I persevered with the policy of inclusion and tried to negotiate with him about presenting a unified front for the Championships. It proved difficult, so I eventually opted for just transferring enough funds to significantly contribute to the payment of flights and

Taking my 6th dan, with Peter looking on from behind, Nottingham, UK, March 2013.

accommodation for him and his two students. I then booked the flights for the remaining squad members and left it at that.

Shortly after, the JKS announced there would be a senior dan examination on the Monday following the championships. This announcement was followed by hearing on the grapevine that Fergus would be grading to 6th dan. He would be more than due at that time and although my allotted waiting time had passed over a year ago, I lived in a world where I couldn't grade unless Yumoto Sensei asked me to. Fergus didn't and was about to take advantage of it. In many ways it didn't bother me; if he graded before me it wouldn't affect my position or career. However, in other ways it bothered me hugely. It just wasn't done and it was an obvious, unsubtle ploy, but I was unsure to what end. This was my ego and I had to let it go.

Others weren't so accommodating. William Sensei from South Africa heard about Fergus's planned leap-frogging of the karate hierarchy and decided to intervene. He contacted me and asked if I was able to change my flights to Japan to allow me to grade. They were non-changeable, non-refundable. He then asked if I would be seeing Yumoto Sensei before then. Of course I would, at our annual Spring Technical Seminar. He instantly went to work. He contacted Takahashi Sempai first, explaining the situation and insisting I grade in the March. He got a quick answer back saying that all 6th dan gradings and above can only take place in Japan.

He countered that the JKS by-laws state that any graduate of the Instructors' Course can get special dispensation to grade anywhere. Takahashi Sempai contacted me immediately and screamed down the phone that I should stop telling lies about my graduation. I said '*osu*' for as long as possible until I had a chance to tell him I had not instigated this campaign, it was coming from William Sensei and other seniors within Europe. He didn't care and hung up on me.

A week later William Sensei forwarded me an email from the Headquarters acknowledging my right to grade anywhere and that I would be allowed to test in March. Such was the complex web of relations, alliances and loyalties at the Headquarters that I have no idea who made the final decision; but my Instructors' Course status was acknowledged and I was given permission.

The weekend arrived, I assisted and taught on the Saturday with the secret knowledge I would be grading straight after training. The course was packed, with 150 members of all four nations present. Peter had been given the job of grading the 1st dan and 2nd dan candidates and Stewart sat with Yumoto Sensei as the 3rd dan and above candidates got ready. We were called to line up and there was an audible 'oooh' as I took my place in the line. It then dawned on me that I had just spent over a decade standing in front of thousands of students, telling them what to do about all things karate. Junior and senior members of the group now looked on and I knew that they had to be thinking 'go on, prove yourself'.

The 3rd dan and 4th dan candidates were immediately called up. As the 5th dan candidate and I readied ourselves for the inevitable fight ahead, Fergus appeared from nowhere.

'Are you grading?' he blurted out, unable to hide his loathing. I nodded, trying to remain focused. 'I can grade,' he continued.

'No, you can't.' I tried to cut the conversation short.

'Yes, I can,' he continued. 'I am due. I can go and get changed now.' It was only then that I realized he wasn't even in his karate suit.

'No, you can't. Sorry.'

'Why not?' He was getting more agitated. 'I'm due. I've done my time. Why can't I grade?'

'Fergus, you can't grade *because you're not me*!' I hissed with a pissed-off finality. He walked away, feeling hard done by, marginalized and under-appreciated. He wanted it so much, to be as senior as me. For him that would make all the difference. If he had considered it for even the shortest of time, he would have realized I was only the eighth-highest-ranking member of the JKS GB & Ireland. Due to the massive influx of good people over the years, seven other members of the group outranked me. Rank wasn't everything.

I quickly tried to focus on the task at hand. I was immediately called up. I fought, just one fight, and then did two *kata*. I passed. Stewart came up to me first.

'Do you want to know what score you got in *kata*?'

'Yeah, sure.' I had passed, so why not?

'6.5,' Stewart informed me. Wow, I thought, that's the highest I had ever seen Yumoto Sensei give anyone. Nick Heald, a tough 6th dan who had come over from the KUGB with Matt Price, arrived.

'Mr Langley …' He always got formal when he was about to compliment me. 'That was very impressive.' I was happy to get praise from such a warrior. Others quickly followed and I allowed myself a brief moment of satisfaction. Then I went to find Peter.

'So, what do you think?' He was the only person whose opinion I asked for.

'Well, it was a bit scrappy … but well done for passing.' He was such a heart-sink, and, I suppose, the perfect antidote to my contentment. However, as my happiness eroded away, I began to consider what had just happened. Since grading for

5th dan six years ago, I always thought that that would be the last grading I would take with the JKS. Not from any desire to grade elsewhere, but due to the increasing complications with my relationship to Japan and Takahashi Sempai. I was shocked I had got this far, but kept that hidden from the vast majority of members. In fact, only Peter and Stewart knew the amount of negotiations, incriminations and ill-feeling that had come about from me testing. For the onlookers, for the faithful and dedicated membership, this was just a natural conclusion of years of hard work. 'Well deserved' was the common response to my upgrading. To them it was simply the JKS acknowledging all my hard work. Little did they know it was given through gritted teeth.

My diploma took ages to arrive because Takahashi Sempai refused to use the term 'Hombu Dojo' when sending mail to the dojo. Instead he just gave the street name. It was one of a multitude of things that just kept making things harder and harder to deal with.

Three months later we all found ourselves in Japan for the JKS World Championships. For me, it was a flying visit with Palma and part of the national team. In recent years Fergus had taken to replicating my 'Japan Trip' and brought anyone willing along on his version of the adventure. The last time I brought him to Japan, in 2009, two of his students had accompanied him and I could feel how uncomfortable he had been in a group led by me. On my trips I always scheduled in a trip to Kabukichō, the safest red-light district you will ever encounter. We would wander the streets late on a Friday night as drunk salarymen staggered from *izakaya* to hostess bar whilst permed *Yakuza*[1] looked on with authority.

1. *Yakuza* – Japanese mafia that have a look all of their own. No one dares tell them they look ridiculous.

On this particular occasion we stumbled across a Pachinko Parlour, so I drew everyone's attention to it and set about explaining how these machines, reminiscent of 1950s vertical pinball machines, were the Mecca of gambling in Japan. Some punters were professional players, but as gambling was illegal in Japan they played to win something incidental, which was then exchanged for cash at a small window adjacent to the parlour. As I explained all this to my enthralled group, I noticed Fergus out of the corner of my eye – he had taken his two students aside and was giving them the rundown on all things Pachinko. As this was only his second visit to Japan I presumed there wasn't much depth to his information. Since then, he had developed greater faith in his ability to negotiate the archipelago and was now responsible for the planning, booking, management and the 'Japan Experience' of his group – and he couldn't speak a word of the lingo!

Back to 2013 and half of the Irish team wandered the streets like proper tourists as I took a trip down memory lane. I even dragged them up to Aiden-Akatsuka, the 'village' I had lived in during the torturous years of the Instructors' Course. I was a little dismayed to find that not only had they changed the name of the station, but also the *gaijin* house, where I had lived all that time ago, had been knocked down – all remnants of my past erased. Things change, especially after eleven years. However, I was glad my local *izakaya* still remained and was capable of facilitating my drunkenness.

Over the weekend Fergus competed and won the Veteran Kata title again. He was undeniably good and I was happy for JKS Ireland, but knew the consequences of such a win on the victor's ego. But I was sad for Mark, my French-Moroccan *kohai*. Over the years I had watched him follow his dream. He had entered the Instructors' Course and successfully graduated. He had then moved back to Morocco and was trying to set up the JKS in the area. I had invited him to Ireland and the UK every year since he graduated and was trying to continue to support him as I had done in Japan. He had become stronger and sharper whilst in Japan, but now that he had left, he still seemed to carry the weight of the Instructors' Course on his shoulders. I looked at him during the competition. He was super strong, energetic and solid. He had text-book karate and created terrific power, but where was the spark? Where was the dynamic explosion of talent? He came second to Fergus, who was almost ten years his senior. Silver in the World Championships is a great result, but I doubt the Instructors' Course gave Mark the karate he desired. He had sweated and bled for four years on the course only to be beaten by Fergus. I felt sorry for him but hoped he could find his way.

That evening the unified Irish team found themselves in a little *izakaya*, tucked away in the streets of Tokyo. Fergus's guys ooh-ed and ahh-ed as various off-menu dishes arrived. I ordered *nomihou-dai* for everyone and we had a great night. Fergus was on form: witty, funny and charismatic, flush from his success that day. We sat next to each other in this small, intimate venue.

'Sempai,' he said, genuinely moved. 'What a great day.'

'To Fergus Sensei ... *Kampaaai*!' I responded, with equal sincerity. Why couldn't it always be this way?

The next day I heard that both Mark and Fergus had passed 5th dan and 6th dan. I was happy for Mark, as they both deserved it. I was also pleased to hear that Mark had sought and achieved revenge when he fought Fergus in the grading. The jovial atmosphere between Fergus and I the night before, I knew, wouldn't make it back to Ireland.

The flying visit was a huge success. Added to this, Yumoto Sensei had summoned me during the Championships. When I found him, Koga, my *kohai* who had rampaged through my guys before the 2007 World Championships in Okinawa, was standing with Yumoto Sensei. In recent years Koga had graduated the course, entered the Japanese National All-Styles Team and had won the World Championships. He was the golden boy of the JKS and Yumoto Sensei's star pupil. Now almost thirty he was retiring from competition to focus on his teaching career. Yumoto Sensei wanted to know if I would employ him for a year or two, giving him a chance to learn English and teach the European affiliates. I immediately said yes as my mind went into hyper-drive. I walked away desperately trying to figure out how I could afford another instructor.

On our return to Japan I looked at the finances of the dojo. There was no way we could afford another full-time instructor's salary, so I developed a plan. I knew that I could start three, maybe four children's beginner classes for Koga. Initially this wouldn't make any money, especially as his English was so low level and he would haemorrhage students. But I was prepared to make the financial investment and knew if he started in September, by the time we had our second big intake of the academic year in January, he would be up to speed and students would be retained. In the meantime, I needed JKS England & Wales and JKS Scotland to take some of the financial burden. I spoke to Peter and Stewart and asked if they would guarantee Koga's employment once a month for a weekend seminar at various clubs up and down the country. This would give him half of a liveable salary. Despite not having the students, my dojo would provide the other half of the salary and we could do this for six months until the Hombu Dojo had built up enough students to warrant a fourth full-time instructor.

I was very excited. I was prepared to leverage my business for him because it would become my exit strategy. Koga was brilliant, a great technician, a formidable fighter and, when not being told to hit people by Sueki, he was a genuinely nice guy. JKS GB & Ireland would love him, and I thought if I could convince him that a life in the West was far more favourable than the suppressive East, I would hand over control of the group to him. I planned to do fifteen years of building the JKS GB & Ireland and in 2017 hand over everything to Koga. My legacy, my organization, would be secured.

When I spoke to Stewart he was as enthusiastic as I was. His dojo in Dunfermline had grown tremendously. He had a regular Sunday afternoon session with a hundred black belts packed into the massive facility. He had forty affiliated clubs that would bite his hand off to have Koga visit them. He instantly saw the value of such a move.

I spoke to Peter, who wasn't as enthusiastic. He questioned the motivation of the Headquarters, if they were sending him over to take control of the jewel in the JKS crown. I tried to appease him. I wasn't stupid: my business would hold control of Koga's visa. Any major issues would result in me sending him packing back to Japan. I had also insisted that any matters involving JKS GB & Ireland must still come through me, and Koga mustn't be used as a liaison for our group. Peter wasn't convinced and refused to play a part in my plan.

The JKS GB & Ireland had never had a chief instructor. Yumoto Sensei was the World Chief Instructor. I was the JKS GB & Ireland Technical Director. That was enough. But Peter had recently taken to calling himself JKS England & Wales Chief Instructor. It was his answer to his anxiety about his position in the group. I stupidly didn't nip it in the bud, and I think his reaction to 'Koga Plan A' was a further deepening of his anxiety. The evidence was all around. Several months earlier at our annual summer camp, I had barely unpacked the car and as my daughter ran around the *Faulty Towers*-esque B&B and a white-gloved proprietor followed her about with wipes, dustpan and brush, Peter insisted we 'have a word'. I followed him knowing it'd be more than one.

'Dan wants to become a grading examiner.' Dan was his one remaining young gun from all those years ago. He had stuck with Peter through thick and thin, had grown up, become 3rd dan and was eligible to be a grading examiner.

'Cool,' I said, knowing Peter didn't share my feelings.

'I'm sorry, but it just isn't on. He doesn't have a club, why does he need to be an examiner?' Dan had recently started getting invited to teach at other clubs. He could deliver Peter's knowledge without the trepidation and elevated petrol costs that befell the host.

'Well, they aren't the rules. The rules are anyone who is 3rd dan and above can take the written test and become an examiner.' I knew we were headed for an argument. Dan taught every time Peter was a no-show, a habit he hadn't gotten out of since the days when Simon had given up attending his dojo. Dan was dedicated, talented and the future of our group. 'Why wouldn't we allow him to grade students?' I concluded.

'There isn't enough to go around as it is, let alone with another examiner.' Wow – there it was. Finally he had verbalized what he had been thinking for years. If Peter felt Dan was a threat, maybe he thought the arrival of Koga was Armageddon.

I rang Stewart to give him the Peter news.

'Fine,' Stewart said, 'I'll take Koga every week.' I'm glad

an international phone line separated us because I could have kissed him. 'Koga Plan B' was put into operation and the plan was for him to teach every Monday and Tuesday in Scotland and then Wednesday and Thursdays in Ireland, leaving the weekends for him to travel and teach around Europe. It was a hard schedule, but I assured Koga it would only be short term. As soon as the dojo could sustain his entire salary, we would revert back to 'Koga Plan A', albeit without Peter being involved.

Koga arrived at the beginning of September and before jet lag had left his body entirely, he was in a new dojo surrounded by new recruits eager to learn how to be ninjas. Of course, I didn't abandon him entirely. I mentored him for two weeks: that is to say, I taught the classes for two weeks as he watched, panic-stricken from the farthest, darkest corner of the dojo. After the fortnight, I came to a decision and told him.

'*Kiyomizu no butai kara tobi oriru tsumori de,*' I said. There was a look of confusion on his face, not because my Japanese was bad, but because my Japanese was good. It was a fairly specialized idiom. Kiyomizu is a well-known temple in Kyoto, which has a famously high stage. The sentence translates as 'by the plan of jumping from the stage of Kiyomizu' and what it actually means is that one must do something with the gusto that it takes to hurl oneself off a high stage. It's much more than just 'taking the plunge'.

He looked at me with an acknowledgment of what must be done. I left him to it, sink or swim. He coped very well and although I was constantly getting phone calls enquiring what the English was for *O-kane* (money), *Doa* (door), *Karate* (karate), he made progress and, thankfully, was cutting his teeth on willing and patient kids. He settled in with the seniors of the dojo too. A couple of the younger guys at morning training buddied up with him, showing him the sights and highlights of Dublin. On Thursday evenings we would take him for a few pints before he would head off at weekends to various JKS affiliates – invites came in thick and fast, including a load from JKS England & Wales dojos. Excellent, I thought. People liked him and he seemed to settle in almost immediately.

One evening, over post-training pints, I explained to him my thoughts on finding a third way within karate organizations and my exit strategy. I felt like the constant dealing with the various elements of the JKS had been a marathon of diplomacy. Similar to many marathon runners, I felt near collapse as I approached the finish line. I had also made progress with my manuscript for *Karate Stupid.* I had finished it back in 2007. Peter and most of the senior members of the JKS GB & Ireland had read it, but beyond that, not much more had happened. I had a literary agent in the UK, but close to retirement, he seemed to have been just sitting on it. I had recently found an agent in Ireland who was willing to represent me. He had it edited and progress was being made. My career by the autumn of 2013 was manic, teaching forty weekends per year at big, international events. Apart from dealing with Peter, Fergus and Takahashi Sempai, it was perfect. However, I thought by publishing my book I could further reduce my involvement with the running of the JKS GB & Ireland and simultaneously reduce the stress of my working life. I wasn't naive enough to believe that I could replace the hard work of weekend seminars with the publication of one book – I knew the arse had fallen out of the publishing industry in recent years, but I also knew it would increase my stock in Europe and cement my position as a professional instructor – plus I wanted to tell my story.

So, after a few pints at the dojo local, I set out my plan

to Koga. He seemed shocked that I would leave the group behind.

'So who will take over if you step down?' he asked.

'Well … you, if you want it.'

'Really?' He seemed genuinely mystified. This simply didn't happen in Japan. Leaders stayed on – forever. Here was I wanting to walk away at the height of the JKS GB & Ireland's success. I tried to explain that for me, it wasn't the power, it was the legacy. I wanted to do something well and have it last. I saw the dynamic nature of people in their thirties and forties. Whether it be work, hobbies or family life, people have fresh energy and ideas as they approach midlife. Maybe in their fifties they can enjoy the fruits of their labour, but I didn't want to be in my sixties, still managing people, still coordinating events, still massaging egos and still walking the tightrope of my precarious position in Japan. Who has that sort of energy? No, I saw Koga's presence in Ireland as a way of slowly moving away. I wouldn't do it overnight, but I knew I could take a step back. I finished with saying that there was no pressure, and if it wasn't him then it would be someone else from Japan, one of our *kohai*. He sipped his pint, deep in thought.

At the start of October Takahashi Sempai made a return to our group. He taught in the UK and he was fantastic. Reminiscent of the first time he had visited our group exactly a decade earlier, he delighted and dazzled everyone in attendance whilst being genuinely nice. With nearly 150 members, the camp was a huge success and what we had become used to – a far cry from his first visit, which was on a wing and a prayer. At that time, 90 per cent of attendees were non-JKS, and now the stats had been reversed. Walking through the dojo was a constant stream of 'Hey' and '*Osu*' as I greeted familiar and friendly faces. At the end I had a chance to sit quietly with Takahashi Sempai and we chatted about JKS events. He had just come back from Mexico, gone straight on to the UK, so he must have been exhausted.

'So where next?' I enquired.

'Well, next year I am with you guys in Scotland and Ireland.' He had already been booked for the March. 'And then … I think I am going to Russia in the summer.'

Wow, I thought. That's it? Takahashi Sempai was like me. He thrived on those short, intense periods of weekend seminars. A chance to be a little bit famous for a little bit of time. Adoration in the right amount, cut short just before you started demanding M&Ms, red only, in your changing room.

He was head of the International JKS Affiliate section and I was surprised he wasn't doing more courses, more of what he wanted. He now had a regular gig with us again. Mexico had him annually. I hoped Russia would be confirmed too. We ended the conversation as I had to take the flight back to Dublin. We stood.

'Is it okay if I hug you?' he asked.

'*Osu*'… always just say *osu*! I stood there, frozen by his humanity. After all these years had we finally reconciled: not reconciled our differences, but reconciled our similarities? I walked away with a smile. Maybe dealing with Japan wasn't as bad as I thought.

My schedule was always busiest in the autumn. I wouldn't have a weekend off from the first weekend in September until the weekend before Christmas. This year was made even worse by the planned trip to Japan slap bang in the middle of my weekend-seminar marathon. The result was that the fortnight trip was reduced to twelve days so I only missed one weekend. I flew to Japan and bounded into the Headquarters with a spring in my step that I had never felt before. Takahashi Sempai greeted me with equal warmth, albeit without the hug. I had a good crew with me and everyone was ready and willing to train hard. At the end of the first session I asked Takahashi Sempai about one of our members. Mike, a very senior 5th dan, was hoping to grade. He was actually one of my original instructors and I had known him since I was a kid. I was delighted to bring him to Japan and wanted to do right by him. I had sent an email about the situation before I arrived and as many members of my group had done a similar thing on previous trips, I didn't expect a problem.

'No, he can't grade,' Takahashi Sempai dictated. 'Tell him he should come back in December and grade on the international course.' The JKS had taken to holding an international course every year on the first weekend of December. I had never been as it was always the same weekend that I invited Peter over to Ireland to help teach, grade my students and be given a thick envelope of cash. However, I heard I wasn't missing much in comparison to coming to the more intermittent Headquarters training.

'Sensei, I don't think he can come again in six weeks' time,' I said, hoping for compassion.

'Well, next year then,' he countered with a certain finality.

I contemplated arguing the point. Not only had members from JKS GB & Ireland graded at the headquarters over the years, everyone who had made the effort to travel to Tokyo had been allowed to grade. It was no inconvenience to attend the morning session at 10.30 a.m. and then grade immediately afterwards when all instructors were present and getting ready for Instructors' Training at midday. However, my relationship with Takahashi Sempai was on the up. As much as it grated, I had to sacrifice Mike's grading for the greater good.

'I'm sorry Mike Sensei, you can't grade,' I said with genuine sorrow. 'Yumoto Sensei won't be at the dojo all week so he can't grade you.' I concluded with genuine sadness that I had been forced to lie to one of my instructors and friends.

Following our time in Tokyo, we made our way to Yokose Sensei's dojo, enjoyed his unfathomable depths of hospitality and then moved on to Okinawa, for the first time since the World Championships six years ago. We landed in the tropical paradise and walked along Kokusai Dori, thankful to be in shorts and flip-flops. I had arranged to train with Senaha Sensei, a 73-year-old Goju-Ryu 9th dan. It was truly magical, training with a gentleman who had learnt from Yagi Meitoku Sensei, who had learnt directly from the founder of the style, Miyagi Chojun Sensei. His dojo, half training space, half living room, perfectly summed up the nature of karate in this small chain of islands. The people were friendly, humorous, compassionate and tough. I had wanted to go for many years and used this annual trip as an excuse. I wanted to see the differences between the two styles. All I saw were similarities. Physically, the fundamental principles were identical, which gave me more insight than if I had found differences. However, the atmosphere in the dojo was in such stark contrast to the schools in the mainland. This, too, was significant. Overall, it was the best trip I had taken to Japan.

I returned with increased vigour and energy for my karate. Plans to ingratiate Koga to the group were moving forward and I could see the light at the end of the tunnel. And it was in this drunken, utopian view of the world that I thought it would be a good idea to send my manuscript of *Karate Stupid* to the Headquarters for their approval.

A week later I heard from the chief instructor of JKS

Mexico. He wondered if I was free the following October. Eleven months hence, I was able to give him a free weekend and a course was quickly arranged. It occurred to me that Takahashi Sempai had been visiting Mexico every autumn for several years, but I guess they felt like a change. Similar things had happened over the last few years in the US, Germany, Portugal and a few other countries. Dark clouds began to gather over my new Utopia, but, busier than ever, I had no time to dwell on such matters. I made my way to the JKS GB Open Championships. Over the last decade it had become one of the best-run championships on the circuit. It was always busy. The night before, Nick Held had convinced me to crowbar the word 'aardvark' into my opening monologue when I told the audience where the emergency exits were, warned competitors about complaining, and basically showed them who was boss throughout the emotionally charged championships.

Looking grumpy after talking to Peter at the JKS GB Open Championships, Nottingham, UK, November 2013.

'So,' I stood, booming to the three or four hundred people present. 'On the aardvark-assions that you may wish to complain, please come and see me directly. Do not complain directly to the referees!'

Nick sniggered behind me. I left the matted areas, with the competitors ready to start.

'Can I have a word?' Peter asked. Here we go, I thought. 'The JKS is doing really well now, so I want a salary.'

'For what?' I could barely contain my incredulity.

'Well, everyone is getting their bit' – by this he meant Matt and Nick, who coached and managed the squad; the money facilitated competition expenses – 'so it's my turn to get some'.

'Yeah … for what?'

'Well, I am chairman.' Apparently he had found meaning to the title.

'You want to be paid for being chairman?'

'Exactly. If I don't get it,' he concluded, 'I walk.'

My worst trait is how manipulative I can be. Peter was my friend. I couldn't authorise him taking the amount he had insisted upon from the JKS GB account each year, but nor did I want him to walk. How could I manage this situation? I spotted Terry, an instructor who had recently been to Japan with me. I hadn't known him well before, but we had chatted a lot during the trip. He had started at the same dojo as Peter around the same time. They went back a long way and I knew Terry and I were both on the same page regarding Peter's idiosyncratic behaviour. I confided in him about the latest revelation. Within the hour, Peter stormed over to me.

'Why the hell are you telling Terry about our private conversation?'

'Peter, think about it. I presume Terry wasn't completely enthralled with the idea of you getting paid from license fee money for just being you. He's your friend. What do you think the general membership would say if they found out? And believe me, they will.' I saw a glimmer of recognition in his face, so I pushed on. 'I'm really busy. Stewart is manic with his dojo. Matt is teaching all over. Why don't we offer you to JKS GB clubs for half price and then the JKS GB account can pay the other 50 per cent?'

'Fine,' he said, and walked off. For fuck's sake! Another bullet dodged.

Dejected, I made my way home. Would it ever end? Weekends like this were hugely financially rewarding, but at what cost? What was driving me to constantly put up with this shite? I loved Peter like a big brother. Did I fear his rejection? Did I fear the rejection of the group? I made my way to the dojo, tucked myself into my office and opened my laptop. I checked my emails and saw one from JKS Headquarters. The subject was 'MANUSCRIPT'.

NINE

Over recent years emails from the Headquarters had become anonymous, simply signed *Headquarters Instructors*. They seemed to be irritated by me *en masse*. Like some house guest who had overstayed their welcome, trivialities such as 'I can't believe he's left his dirty dishes in the sink again' were endlessly highlighted, rather than simply saying 'Get the fuck out of my house!' Unsigned emails arrived with regular monotony:

> *Dear Scott Sensei,*
> *Yumoto Sensei's return flight arrived at 6 a.m. the Tuesday after your seminar with him – you should have paid him for this day also. Transfer the funds immediately.*
> *Headquarters Instructors*

> *Dear Scott Sensei,*
> *You gave Yumoto Sensei money for the dan rank test he conducted at the seminar. This money must be transferred electronically, you should not expect him to do your job for you.*
> *Headquarters Instructors*

> *Dear Scott Sensei,*
> *When you arrive at seminars with international JKS affiliates, if you are asked to conduct a dan rank exam you must ask for permission one month before your arrival.*
> *Headquarters Instructors*

However, the email I received late November was different. I opened it up and effectively pressed start on the most intense month of my life. Yuri, the Russian-born, trilingual secretary of the JKS had at least signed his name and taken ownership, differentiating it from the recent glut of ghostwritten correspondence. He asked for a convenient time to call that day. I emailed him back, saying I was free any time and to just call. Five minutes later I saw the 'withheld' line come up on my phone – always Japan.

'*Mushi Mushi*!' although I always spoke to Yuri in English, I liked to give the impression I was psychic.

'Hi, is that Scott Sensei?' We spent a few minutes being Japanese in our politeness, putting off the inevitable.

'Scott Sensei,' he commenced. 'You are an icon in Europe.' He actually used those words. I laughed, and then became quiet when I realized he was serious. 'You cannot publish this book,' he continued, not feeling the need to explain why. 'Also, I have a personal reason why I would like you not to publish. I am the only *gaijin* at the Headquarters now. I have spent many years building my stock here.' I was glad I wasn't the only one who thought in such terms. 'If you publish this book it will destroy everything I have worked for.'

I didn't quite agree with him. Of course, the premise that the book reflected badly on the JKS was the first and, really, only element of the disagreement that mattered. He read the book with his Russian sense of humour, his Russian understanding of English and his Russian desire to suppress individuality. I tried to convince him that many native English speakers had read the book and found it fine – Peter, Stewart and Mark, amongst others, had really liked it. I also let him know that this project had gone so far down the road of publication that it was too late to stop. Of course, this wasn't entirely true, but in my heart it was. I had poured my soul into this work, so how could I kill it off?

Apparently he had been tasked by Takahashi Sempai to read the book and give his verdict to the Headquarters. They would take his lead as none of them could speak English to any great level. He suggested I make a few changes and then he would give his approval. I left the conversation, with him asking me to send a soft copy of the manuscript. He would then give me his feedback, I could make changes and would receive his approval. As I slipped the phone back in my pocket I felt a sense of dread. This wasn't going to end well.

Over recent years Peter, Stewart and I had taken to meeting every last Tuesday of November. We would change country each year and the host would be responsible for accommodation, whilst the two travellers paid for their flights. We would find a suitable location, have lunch, talk about the coming year's schedule, thrash out any issues (aka dealing with matters arising from Peter's leadership) and then get drunk. This year we met in Leicester and luckily Stewart's self-imposed drinking ban only applied to Scotland, so we set out on a pub crawl of the city centre. Several libations into the night, I brought up my recent conversation with Yuri. Peter just shrugged. He had read the book several years earlier and couldn't see the issue with it. Stewart suggested I publish it under a *nom de plume*. I was more impressed by his use of

French than the merits of his idea. That wouldn't work. It was my story, I wanted to take ownership of it, not distance myself. We finished the drunken evening with an, 'Ah, it'll be grand. What's the worst that could happen?'

On my return from Leicester I found an email from Yuri. He had been a busy boy. He explained that he had highlighted in red everything he felt I should have a look at, requesting that I consider changing the wording or toning down the narrative. He had then highlighted in red with bold text everything that he felt I must delete or dramatically change from the manuscript. I clicked on the Word document and found a sea of bold red. *Karate Stupid* was very red and very bold, and the first two words of the book were out: not a good start.

I scanned the rest of the manuscript and it quickly became apparent that in order to gain his approval, my book would have to be significantly rewritten. The list was endless: I couldn't mention that I had been fingerprinted when I received my resident identification; I had to delete my reference to beating an old granny to a seat on the train; I couldn't write Takahashi and tormentor or nemesis in the same sentence; I couldn't admit to telling any lies when I was on the course; I had to delete all references to my emotional state; oh, and I couldn't mention the Second World War. John Cleese would have been proud.

I spent the next few heartbreaking weeks deleting passages, changing words, toning down references to violence and turning my loved and manicured work into an ugly, cumbersome account of no real significance. I sent the all-new *Karate Gaijin* to Yuri, hoping it would put this problem to bed, but also wishing it didn't. I had no real desire to publish the desecrated, dishonest version of my story.

This was the busiest time of year. The first weekend of December Peter was in Dublin earning his yearly bonus from JKS Ireland. The following week I was over in England teaching the Christmas course there. I was weighed down with stress, having also picked up a knee injury that, unsurprisingly, I couldn't shake. On the Saturday morning I woke up, unable to eat breakfast, and threw up as we were leaving for the dojo. Unsure what was wrong with me, I brushed my teeth and headed to the waiting car, determined to do a good job.

I couldn't move dynamically at all, so set about teaching from natural stance, trying to get people to move away from making shapes, and implementing the principles of karate. Two hours later, dripping in sweat and completely spent, Matt Price and other seniors of the group graciously nodded their approval.

'That was a great class!' Claire, the secretary of *Shotokan Karate Magazine*, came bounding up afterward. 'Brilliant – shapeless karate. Can you write an article?'

It had been a while since I had written a technical article for the magazine, but after a decade of trying to find my way whilst nicking a whole load of ideas from Steve Ubl, I thought I had finally inched forward. The article wrote itself and was sent shortly afterwards. I walked out of the dojo. I had finally broken free of the constraints of Shotokan karate, the JKS method, and the system, in every format. *Shu-Ha-Ri*![1]

The following evening I stayed with Simon. It had become tradition that I taught for him the Monday after the Christmas course. We drank and I talked about the situation. At this point no one else knew of the pending disaster and I was

1. *Shu-Ha-Ri* is a well-used Japanese idiom, which refers to the natural progression of a martial artist. *Shu* means obey, *Ha* means detach and *Ri* means leave. Every child must eventually grow up.

unsure how people would react.

'Oh, God, I hope they don't force you out of the JKS,' he said with all the gloom and despair I felt. 'Because that'll mean I'm out too.' It was the first time I really considered what would happen if I left. I didn't want to force people to choose.

'I've found these for you.' The next morning I was greeted by a frantic Simon in the full swing of an energetic whirlwind. He had a truly extensive martial arts library and had been busy since dawn. 'Look at this!' He shoved *A Slow Boat to Yokohama* under my blurry eyes. 'Or this … he's Japanese': *The Human Face of Karate.* 'And don't forget Stan Schmidt's *Spirit of the Empty Hand.*'

He had found a whole bunch of references to the violence that percolates traditional Japanese martial arts. Stan Schmidt had written extensively about it and he had been promoted to 8th dan *and* had been head of the JKA in South Africa. His honesty certainly hadn't been frowned upon. I taught that night, thankful of Simon's friendship, and left the next day armed with various book references just in case I had to defend my position.

Several days later another delightful email arrived in my inbox: *You have changed nothing* – I could imagine Yuri stabbing his keyboard as he typed – *You will leave me with no choice but to translate certain passages and inform Takahashi Sempai of the lies you told.*

I rang him. 'What lies?'

'You lied about going home at Christmas in the first year and about your uncle's death in the second year.' He was outraged about two white lies from over a decade ago.

'Well, ironically, I am being honest about those lies.'

'What do you mean, "ironically"?' That kind of summed up everything. He ended the conversation rather ominously: 'You leave me no choice!'

I didn't know this at the time but Yuri set about cherry-picking certain passages, translating them and presenting them to the instructors. *Takahashi Sempai was my nemesis, my tormentor* became *Takahashi Sempai was the spirit of retribution and a torturer*. And *Sueki was the only Teikyo student stupid enough that year to enter the Instructors' Course* became *Sueki is stupid*. I am sure it was easy for him to take certain passages and present them in a way that portrayed my book in an entirely different light. Of course, the book was honest and presented my life on the course, warts and all. However, it was my life. In many ways it was a love letter to Japan. The narrative was my rite of passage. It presented the course like many others have presented elite training processes. Read any story of SAS selection and you can't help but think the journey of a candidate is arduous in the extreme. This doesn't undermine the regiment and in many ways it reinforces existing, accurate beliefs. No one in the karate world believed that the Instructors' Course was easy. Stories of some of the Western pioneers of karate who had taken part in instructors' training in the 1970s and 1980swere circulated with great relish. As early as 1975 C.W. Nicol in *Moving Zen* had talked about such extreme training. Stan Schmidt Sensei went on to tell the story of 'Bullet Head' jumping on the back of his training partner and biting off his ear! Descriptions of violence on the course could be read at length with a simple Google search. However, when the translated highlights of my book were presented, I doubt Yuri put things into context; after all, he had his own personal reasons for not wanting the book published.

The response was immediate and angry. Takahashi Sempai phoned – it was possibly the first time he had called me directly since I left Japan and it would also be the last time I would speak to him. He was outraged.

'How can you say these things?' he demanded.

'But Sensei, if you read the whole book you will understand. Please ask Mark, he has read the book and thinks it's fine.' I had spoken to Mark. Still working hard in Morocco, we had been in constant communication about this issue as they had contacted him when they had received the manuscript. Educated at an English-speaking school, he was one of the few native speakers they could trust.

'I have spoken to him, and he agrees with me!' he screamed. How can that be? Mark had read the book years before and had no issue. He also had no issue two days earlier, when we had last spoken. 'Did you mention my elbow in the book?' Takahashi Sempai was referring to his right elbow. He had suffered for years from joint calcification and had undergone several operations, one of which had been halfway through my time on the course, giving me a much-needed reprieve from my nemesis.

'Yes, Sensei, I did, and you tell students about your elbow on every course you teach.' He had reduced mobility in the joint and didn't want students to copy him.

'How dare you. This is private!' Furious, he slammed down the phone with great finality.

Within minutes I was Skyping Mark. His support of Takahashi Sempai and Yuri's position seemed to have tipped the scales, and not in my favour.

'I thought you liked the book.' I was desperate.

'Look, as much as I respect everyone's right to tell their story, I think you should write more about the philosophy of karate. The beauty and depth of Japanese culture. The honour that was bestowed upon us by being allowed to train in the Instructors' Course.'

In recent years I had noticed Mark slowly morph into the person I was talking to now. He had been a giggly innocent when he arrived in Tokyo in 2001, completely unprepared for the JKS World Championships. Now he was a strong graduate of the Instructors' Course, fluent in Japanese and married to a beautiful Japanese lady with three of the cutest kids anyone could hope for. However, in some important ways he was worse than the wide-eyed innocent that arrived in Japan. Now he needed to follow a guru, and was ready to jump as soon as they said how high.

'That's not my book, Mark. That's not the story I want to write, that's the story you want to write.'

He tilted his glasses, the same way Yumoto Sensei did when he was deep in thought. I was talking to someone who was so heavily invested in the Headquarters' reality, that he found it almost impossible to loop out of that closed system – my degree in anthropology was finally paying off. The conversation ended without conclusion and for the last time I said goodbye to a friend I had helped out on many occasions. This, unfortunately, would become a recurring theme from now on.

I fell into JKS purgatory for the next couple of days. It was close to Christmas and I thought nothing would happen until the New Year. However, I didn't want this hanging over my head for the holidays and decided to fly to Japan for a meeting with Yumoto Sensei. It was the only way forward. Takahashi Sempai and Yuri could spin their delightful web of half-truths and cherry-picked fragments of reality, but if I stood in front of Yumoto Sensei, he would see the person he had known for the last quarter of a century. I left it a few days for tempers to calm, then called Yuri, explained my plan and got Yumoto Sensei's schedule for January. I emailed Stewart and Peter, offered to pay for their flights and gave them a midweek date in January when we could all provide a united front. With the whole weight of JKS GB & Ireland behind me, it would go a long way to help the situation. I received a reply from Stewart first: as much as he didn't want to go to Tokyo for two days, he would, if that's what it took. Then Peter emailed: *Sorry mate. I have booked a flight up to Aberdeen that week to see my mum.* He flew up at least every other month and always scheduled it to avail of the cheap EasyJet deals. He wouldn't have paid more than £20 for the flight.

What could I say? I closed my laptop, unable to stop myself from logging all the times and occasions I had helped him out; the times I had appeased certain members who were pissed off with his attitude, the situations I had defused as he stumbled through the political landscape of JKS GB & Ireland like an Aberdeen Angus in a china shop. Despite all our differences, he was my friend. I loved him, and fought on many occasions to defend him and his idiosyncratic ways. Many years ago I had asked him for advice about how to set up a dojo. He had given it freely and gladly. I paid him back by having Yumoto Sensei teach at the dojo. Then I brought him into the JKS and heavily promoted and supported him through the years. We had shared many good times and benefited financially from the growth of the JKS, but I had never asked him for anything until now. I was deeply upset.

The next day, 20 December 2013, I stood in my living room, ironing my clothes. It was Tor's last day of work and early the following day all three of us would be travelling to the UK for

Christmas. As I neatly folded my favourite T-shirt the phone rang. It was Stewart.

'Have you checked your email this morning?'

'No.'

'Check it and call me back.'

I fired up my laptop and opened the email from Headquarters titled *'Disciplinary Action!'*

Dear Mr Langley it began – they never called me Mr Langley. I was either Scott, Scott Sempai or Scott Sensei. I had been suspended. Facing a disciplinary hearing on 26 January 2014 I wasn't allowed to teach karate outside my own dojo in Dublin, conduct any dan or kyu examination or referee or coordinate any competition. Furthermore, Fergus would be made the contact person and head of JKS Ireland. I looked at the address bar and saw the head of every international affiliate had been cc'd into the email. There was a document attached to the email. It set out the reason for my suspension. They seemed to believe that *Karate Stupid* was already on sale, as my suspension was due to the publication of the book after I had promised, but failed, to make major changes in the manuscript. They believed the 'fictitious' book misrepresented the Instructors' Programme and they wanted to set the record straight. They attached a copy of my Shugyosei certificate I had sent them five years ago, and also a copy of Mark's. They pointed out how different they were: mine had been written by Taguchi Sensei, Mark's hadn't. They went on to say I had made 'passionate and constant requests' to enter the course and only after this had they allowed me on in April 2001. However, I was only allowed to become Shugyosei, not Kenshusei, because my karate was low level. It continued. In June 2002 they had 'allowed' me to return home as I had claimed I had financial problems and on my return I had asked for an 'Apprentice Certificate' that the late Taguchi Sensei had kindly fulfilled.

I couldn't believe it. This type of punishment, as far as I was aware, was completely unprecedented. To take a group from someone was unheard of – and I wouldn't have believed even possible. As for their reasoning, their lies were so blatant. I had my invitation letter to enter the Instructors' Course, dated 2 April 2000. My name had been on the instructors' name board at the Headquarters. It had been there for five years until Takahashi Sempai fell out with me. I begged to be allowed on the course and to be certified? It was ludicrous, but in a single email history was dramatically rewritten. Since 2007 Takahashi Sempai had been presenting his fantasy, but now it had been formalized. It was there in black and white.

Over the years leading up to this email, I had thought many times about my graduation. What really happened? Eventually I came to the conclusion that it doesn't really matter. Mark, along with many others, was a graduate of the Instructors' Course and had made little impact in the world of Shotokan Karate. Instructors like Ishii Sensei had never graduated the Instructors' Course, yet had become significant contributors to the lexicon of our beloved style. But I knew what I had done. I hadn't begged to enter the course. Shortly after arriving in Japan, admittedly after some less than subtle hints, Richard Amos has asked me what my intentions were. I spoke about wanting to train harder. This had led to an invitation onto the Instructors' Course, which had been postponed due to injury until the spring of 2000. I had asked no one; I was asked by Yumoto Sensei.

I entered the course and trained hard for two years. They had never wanted another foreigner on the course, and I had fought to win their respect. In so doing I had facilitated Mark to follow in my footsteps. On graduation day, I was sidelined whilst Sueki graduated. Taguchi asked me to do three more months. After two and a half months I asked Yumoto Sensei if he knew when I would graduate – I really did have to get home and start earning money. He gave me a date three weeks hence and I took the examination in front of Taguchi Sensei. A week later we had a graduation party, I was presented with my certificate of completion, 4th dan, and registration certificate of JKS Ireland. On the name board, my name was moved from *Shugyosei* to Instructor. I had graduated, and it remained that way for five years. When asked, Yumoto Sensei talked openly about my time on the course and was proud at how I had persevered and completed it. Takahashi Sempai had been interviewed by *Shotokan Karate Magazine* and talked about the growth of the JKS and how, with the help of instructor course graduates like Koyama in France and Scott in Ireland, he thought the JKS would continue to grow.

I sat dumbfounded in my living room as my iron steamed away, wondering what the hell had just happened. I was forbidden to do karate outside the four walls of my dojo? My mind couldn't settle into a reality where that was even possible. Karate was my life; I thought about little else. How can my sensei and sempai, 9,000 km away, decide where and how I did karate? And how can they take the group from me and give it to Fergus? It wasn't theirs to take or give. I had built the group up literally from the ground. The JKS brand didn't exist in Ireland and hardly existed in Europe before I returned. I couldn't fathom how this could even enter into the possibilities of their response to the issue. I rang Stewart.

'Don't worry,' he said, 'we'll sort this out'. He was obviously having conversations with the Headquarters, but I felt he was still on my side. As I hung up, the phone started ringing again. The number was foreign but I didn't recognize the country code.

'Hello, is that Scott? This is William from South Africa.'

'*Osu*, Sensei. How are you?' I was taken aback that the most senior member of the JKS outside Japan was calling me. We discussed the sudden turn of events.

'So, what will you do? Would you leave the JKS if they suspend you for longer?' I hadn't really considered it. This was all very sudden and I had no contingency plan.

'Sensei, the JKS is my family. I can't even imagine not being part of the group. I've worked too long and too hard to walk away from all this.' It was true. I no longer wanted to run JKS GB & Ireland, but that didn't mean I wanted to leave the JKS. He seemed pleased with my response and I hung up wondering if he had the information he wanted.

The next call followed fairly quickly. It was Jan Spatzek, a 7th dan from Denmark and the most senior member in Europe. Jan Sensei was my karate father. A deeply humble man who oozed karate knowledge, I had known him since I was a kid and we had formed a bond that transcended the time and distance that limited our contact. I fought back tears as I spoke to him. All my defences melted away as I confided in this wonderful man.

'Don't worry, Scott. I won't let this happen. It will be okay.' I mumbled and sniffled a thank you and hung up. The rest of the day was a bit of a blur. Between answering emails, Facebook messages, telephone calls and text messages from the four corners of the JKS world, whilst packing my bag and looking after my daughter, I collapsed on the sofa sometime after 9 p.m., ready for bed and the early start in the morning to catch the ferry.

'What did Peter say?' Tor sat next to me as we shared a bottle of wine. It was only then that it dawned on me that he hadn't made contact at all. Fergus was the only other person who had been cc'd into the email not to contact me, and that was to be expected, but surely Peter would get in touch?

The next morning I was in contact with Stewart again. I mentioned I hadn't heard from Peter and then, twenty minutes later, a text arrived: *Hi mate, I was just giving you some space. If you want to talk, call anytime*. I was already on the ferry, so left it until we docked. Driving through the windy roads of Anglesey I called him, and we had the same conversation I'd had with the other seniors around the world. Then he said, 'Look, you're my mate – whatever you do, you have my 100 per cent support.'

'Thanks mate, that means a great deal. I appreciate it.' I hung up. It would become the last time I ever spoke to him. Twenty-five years of friendship would end with a lie.

Still in a positive, deluded frame of mind, I replied to my '*Disciplinary Action!*' email, thanking them for their comments and that I would reply in the New Year. Shima Sempai responded on Christmas Day, saying I had no need to respond to the letter and I was not to attend the disciplinary hearing. I put it to the back of my mind. They had destroyed Christmas for me before, I was not going to let it happen again.

I returned to work in the New Year. Christmas had been a blur with thoughts of Japan never too far away, ready to destroy any merriment I could muster. I emailed all the clubs in JKS Ireland, who deserved to know Fergus was in charge for the time being. I immediately got panic-stricken messages back. Apparently Fergus had touched base with the majority of dojo heads over the holidays. He never usually had anything to do with most of the group and now he was personally wishing them well and saying, puzzlingly, he had had the best Christmas present ever. Mystery solved!

Thomas, Richard, Harry and the rest of the morning crew were very concerned. During the first week back it became the only topic of conversation, but I assured everyone that I would sort it out. Harry was the most upset and voiced his concerns.

'Don't worry mate. I'm not going to sacrifice the whole of the organization for a book.'

Communications and negotiations intensified in the first two weeks of January. William Sensei, Jan Sensei and Stewart shot emails back and forth to Japan like a demented game of ping-pong. Emotionally exhausted, I also felt completely powerless, but I was deeply grateful that I had friends and sensei I could trust to fight my corner. I never had any courses or events organized in January anyway, so the month-long ban was, in effect, pointless. I just let things play out as they inevitably would.

On 10 January William Sensei rang with news from Japan. If I apologized to Yumoto Sensei for writing the book and the lies I told and promised never to publish it, all would be forgotten and we could move on. What choice did I have? The JKS was my family. The JKS GB & Ireland was my baby. It had grown, through the help of others, to become the biggest single-style organization in the British Isles. I had done that – I couldn't just throw it away. I loved my book, but I also loved the group I had worked so hard to build.

I called Koga to the dojo and we set about writing an email to Yumoto Sensei entirely in Japanese. Koga suggested I write it in English and Yuri would translate, but I needed to cut out the middleman. I also didn't want an email written in English that they – Takahashi Sempai – could use against me at a later date. I composed the email in my clumsy Japanese and Koga put the native speaker's finesse to it. I promised, as a JKS member who had the greater good of the group at heart, not to publish the book. I also apologized for the lies I had told whilst on the Instructors' Course. I knew Takahashi Sempai wanted me to apologize for what I had said about my graduation but they weren't lies. I sent the email.

The next day I received an email directly from Yumoto Sensei, which began with *Dear Scott*. Finally, connection had been re-established. He accepted my email and apology. He felt a lot of damage had been done but my promise not to publish had been well received and he knew that with some work we could put all this behind us. I let out a huge sigh of relief, and the weight of the previous few weeks lifted from my shoulders. Emails arrived from the key figures who had been with me on the road to pardon. They, too, seemed to be filled with the helium of victory. Thank God and *thank fuck for that*! I told the guys in the dojo; Harry immediately sprang to life, as did the others. It was amazing how the stress since the end of November had infected every part of my job, and their hobby. It was generally concluded that it was all over, the disciplinary hearing would be cancelled and we could return to life as it was, as it should be.

The next day I received another anonymous email from the Headquarters. It was addressed to Stewart, Peter, Fergus, myself and, this time, Matt Price. Fergus had been informed about Yumoto Sensei's email and had responded immediately. Was he still in charge? Was the disciplinary hearing still going ahead? Apparently the answer to both questions was yes. But again, all the active players involved thought it was of little consequence. What was interesting was the inclusion of Matt Price. Until this point, he, like the large number of other dojo heads in our group, had not been involved in any of the palaver. Why now? It was obvious. Takahashi Sempai was hedging his bets. He knew Peter and I were close. He may have thought Peter would become an issue as well. Was Matt being set up as the next in charge of JKS England and Wales? Takahashi Sempai had the tactical astuteness of a shotgun, but it didn't bode well. Yumoto Sensei had called an end to this fiasco. Why the disciplinary hearing?

Again, through it all, I had not spoken to Peter once. However, as Matt had been cc'd into the email thread from hell, others in the UK started to get wind of the story. I spoke to a number of dojo heads, friends I had brought into the JKS and supported for many years. I tried to appease their concerns. Those in the know were confident it would all blow over. We just had to wait until 26 January and all this would be buried once and for all. I was unsure how JKS Ireland would look afterwards, because there was no way I could tolerate Fergus in the group anymore, but at least things would return to normal. *Kangeiko* was held the week leading up to Sunday 26. It was always a time I cherished, with a different senior member of my dojo leading the class each day. In recent years I had so many seniors it was impossible to allow everyone to shine, but I was happy that our massive dojo came together once a year. Early on in the week I received a text from Peter: *Are you telling people about the problem? I thought we weren't telling anyone?*

Yeah, tell anyone … tell EVERYONE! I texted back. I meant it. The more that knew about this, the better. I could feel Takahashi Sempai's vision of the future wasn't particularly congruent with Yumoto Sensei's. Peter never replied and I knew he was worried. I was too, but I suspected the outcome I feared and the outcome Peter feared were not the same.

Sunday 26 January eventually arrived. Nearly a hundred enthusiastic members crammed into my little dojo and we set about finishing our week-long ordeal. An hour later, with foggy mirrors and sweaty walls, I handed out completion certificates to the fifty or so die-hards and ordered them to eat, drink and be merry. I had a brief moment of forgetfulness as I toasted everyone and had a sip of my well-deserved alcoholic's early morning beer, then thought I had better check my email. I didn't expect anything until Monday, but wanted to put my mind at rest. I went to my office and fired up my laptop – and there is was, waiting expectantly: *Dear Mr Langley* it started ominously. It was titled *The Sanction against Scott Langley* and went on very rapidly. Signed by Yumoto Sensei and Matsumura Sensei, the JKS Chairman, I was, with immediate effect, suspended from the organization, as were all my JKS licenses and privileges. This would continue until September 2015, one week before the next World Championships, when I would be expected to compete and re-establish my honour in front of the JKS hierarchy. Failure to comply with these sanctions would result in my expulsion from the group. That was it. No mention of the reason for this punishment, no mention of my endeavours to reconcile our differences, no mention of the contribution I had made to the group over the last decade. It was a *fait accompli*.

I closed my laptop, closed my eyes and took a deep breath. For the briefest of moments it wasn't real yet. But in the instant I took my second breath, I could see the consequences of the email pan out in front of me like the fracturing of bullet-proof glass, failing to break, but being forever cracked by the shot. With an acknowledgment of the irony, I reminded myself I had done the Instructors' Course. Like an Etonian falling back on his old-boys' network or a Mason sealing a business deal with a special handshake, the knowledge of what I had done helped spur me on just when I needed it most. I stood up, ready to face my squad, and almost bumped into Harry on leaving the office.

'Well, by the look on your face, it wasn't good news.'

'Yeah, follow me.' I called the guys together. They were already in the throes of the post-*Kangeiko* party but knew I was expecting news. I explained the situation. I was surrounded by my life. Tor and Gayle stood next to me. Harry, Thomas and Richard were there too, the karate buddies that I had always craved. Sharing my love of the art, I was their friend far more than their sensei. Palma and other members of staff huddled in too. I gave them the news. Harry was crestfallen. Richard was very quiet. Thomas just shrugged, indifferent to what the JKS had to say about me. Gayle was outraged: how dare they? Deeply ethical, she was incensed by the hypocrisy of the decision. Everyone was supportive, realizing the ramifications of Japan's decision.

'Okay.' Tor was serious, switched on. 'What do you need to do right now?' Ever since Yumoto Sensei's decisive email hadn't ended this saga, Tor and I had talked about what could happen, hoping for the best, but preparing for the worst. No plans had been firmed up, they were just vague ideas, formless mist in the strategic planning department of my brain.

'Contact John Cheetham and see if I can get an advert for my book in the March issue of *Shotokan Karate Magazine*.'

'Anything else?'

I thought about how things would play out over the next couple of days. 'No, I don't think so.' For now, nothing needed to be done. I went back in my office, sent the email and returned to the party.

I once described the anticipation of pain as being far worse than the pain itself. The stress on the Instructors' Course wasn't caused by the severity of the training, it was the expectancy of the upcoming ordeal that was suffocating. Now, a decade later, the same psychological mechanics were at play. The energy-sapping psychosis that I had had to fight against for a month evaporated in an instant. The pain was over and I could see the future again.

The party in the dojo wound up at about midday. Already drunk, we went for a boozy lunch, followed by afternoon drinks, followed by dinner and an evening out on the town. I staggered and stumbled home late that evening. For most of the day I had been distracted by alcohol and friends from the new ordeal that I now faced, but walking home alone it hit me in a tsunami of emotions. Drunkenly I found myself diving into a pool of self-confidence. 'At least,' I found myself thinking, possibly talking out aloud, 'I can publish my book!' I remember clenching my fist in a slight nod to that victory. I knew that moving forward was going to be tough, but at least I could tell my story.

The following afternoon I emerged from my coma to a message from Stewart, asking how I was and what I was going to do. *I don't know, mate,* I replied, lying. *I have to think about it. But you'll be the first to know.* But there was only really one way forward. It was impossible for me not to work for almost two years. They were punishing me for publishing a book I had promised not to publish. I couldn't be subjugated like this. I didn't deserve it and I had too much self-respect to accept it. I also couldn't hand over to Fergus and Peter the group I had worked so hard to build. I would find it impossible for them to inherit something that they had had little input in creating. In the years they had been members Fergus, had not facilitated one club joining the group. Peter had brought in only one.

I knew there was a karate world out there other than the JKS that was of the highest quality and deepest authenticity. Plus, what is authenticity? My last trip to Japan had taught me this. The JKA denounce the JKS as illegitimate, Taguchi Sensei had lost the court case back in 1999, the JKA were the 'Keepers of the Highest Tradition'. But in Okinawa the masters there denounced mainland karate as illegitimate, devoid of hundreds of years of tradition and knowledge. I am sure there are masters in China, learning the traditions of the Shaolin monks who look at Okinawa dismissively, having lost the internal elements of what once was. And could there be some yogi in India looking at Chinese martial arts and wondering what the hell they are doing, having misunderstood the teachings of Bodhidharma, the hard-living Buddhist monk who brought martial training to China from the subcontinent? For many Japanophiles, the need to be connected to the East was the last bastion of acceptable racism. For me, my blinkers had long ago been yanked away. It was time to move on and there was only one way I would ever go.

Wednesday 29 January was the day to move on. I hadn't done or said anything since receiving the verdict from the Headquarters, but Fergus had called an emergency meeting that coming Sunday. Of course I wasn't invited, so I had to let people know what I was doing before then. I spent all day composing a countless number of emails and saving them in my drafts folder. Every dojo within JKS Ireland, England and Wales had their own email. I wanted to explain to them personally what I was going to do, why I was doing it and, if they wanted, they could follow me. I emailed Stewart, Jan Sensei and William Sensei, thanking them for their support, encouragement and friendship. I finished, holding back the emotion, with composing the emails to Peter and Yumoto Sensei. Peter's was very short. *Your silence speaks volumes* I wrote. *Some will follow me, some will stay with you. Stay well, Scott*. What more was there to say?

But the emotions that I felt towards Yumoto Sensei were articulated with far greater depth. I started by assuring him I had thought long and hard and come to my decision with a heavy heart; that I had worked tirelessly for the last decade to build a group that I, he and the JKS could be proud of, and that I had meant no offence when writing the book and the promise not to publish, as a JKS member, was sincere. However, I chronicled the series of events that had led to first having my name removed from the instructors' board, then my degrading from graduation to completion and the claim that I only trained on the course for a little over a year. I spoke of my sorrow at being treated like this and how, as an adult, as a sensei, as a husband, father, employer – as a man, I couldn't accept this. I resigned from the JKS.

At 5 p.m. that Wednesday, I sent all the emails and posted the following on my Facebook page:

> *It is with great regret that I am resigning from the JKS with immediate effect. On 26 January I was suspended from the group for twenty-two months. I was not allowed to attend the disciplinary hearing, but I feel the punishment was punitive and harsh. It relates to the upcoming publication of my book and that JKS Japan claim*

I never graduated the Instructors' Course. As sorry as I am to leave the group that I have called 'home' for the past thirty years, I am happy to announce that I will be joining Richard Amos Sensei and taking my group into the WTKO.

TEN

It may be just happenstance, but today is 20 December 2015, two years to the day since I was suspended from the JKS. Or maybe it is just another example of how I, consciously or subconsciously, strategically plan and manage my life, wanting to start the last chapter on this date. I am like a mad puppeteer who only really wants to control himself.

I'm sitting in my hotel room in Karlskrona, a small town in South Sweden I have dropped into for the weekend. Like parachute tourists who land in to some generic holiday resort in Spain, Greece, France or Italy, I find myself teaching in yet another dojo, in yet another town, in yet another country. I am tired. I have never worked so hard in my life and this weekend, five days before Christmas, is my last gig of a mammoth year where I have taught fifty seminars over forty-five weekends. But I am also ecstatic. The instructors here are great. – warm, talented and hospitable. I wouldn't be teaching this late in the season for anyone else. I've turned down a few courses this year, but not these guys. I am happy to finish the year on a high. But it hasn't always been like this, and January 2014 was different altogether.

One of the last conversations I had with Peter I remember getting feisty. 'They'll regret it,' I said as we talked about what would happen if they forced me to leave. 'I control the message, they don't.' Maybe I had heard this type of talk on some American TV show or read it in some over-the-top blockbuster. It didn't matter that this wasn't my normal turn of phrase, I meant what I said. The world is ruled by the English language. I understood the power of social media and I knew that it would be my truth that rose to the surface.

I timed the sending of the emails and the posting on Facebook as best as I could, giving me as much time as possible to get my version of events out first. Japan received the emails in the middle of the night and the Western JKS world got the message through Facebook as they made their way home from work or meandered to the dojo. Within a few hours I had over 200 comments on my post and an equal number of private messages. At one point my computer pinged with emails, my mobile pulsed with incoming messages and my screen lit up as members of the JKS world called over concerns of the sudden turn of events. From 5 p.m. until late, my kitchen was a one-man communications hub as I tried to make contact with everyone who reached out to me. I had one chance to make it work. I knew people would be in shock, so I explained my position as best as I could and then left them to it. That first day I had no commitment from anyone, but nor did I expect it. I had to have faith and see what happened. My club would become the WTKO Ireland Hombu Dojo and we would see who followed.

It was a hard time. Koyama Sempai sent a congratulatory messages. *You are now free*, he wrote. Mark's response was the antithesis: he recommended that as Tor had a good job and my daughter was still young, I should return to Japan and finish the course I had started. I was sorry I had let him into my life. Jan Sensei's email was angry, but not at me. *I will always be your friend*, he wrote. I broke down and cried. I was losing so much. I was engulfed by waves of fear and despair.

This was exacerbated by the reaction of the JKS. Koga was immediately ordered to pack up his small apartment and move permanently to Scotland. Fergus had already organized a meeting on Sunday 3 February and Peter followed suit, calling all dojo heads to Leicester. Fergus spouted the party line that I was a liar and had never really graduated from the course. It fell on deaf ears; these guys knew my level. He then further irritated them when he ordered them not to have any contact with me for the next six months, and finished off the meeting by mentioning that he was the only one in Ireland who was officially allowed to do JKS examinations. For years, quite legitimately, anyone 3rd dan and above was allowed to grade their students for colour belts. It was the source of most of the money a dojo or organization could generate. Within the group several instructors were professional due to me giving permission for them to grade their own students, but he was putting that in jeopardy. I was immediately informed and my heart gave a little skip as I knew his form of diplomacy couldn't help but turn most of the members against him.

Peter had a little more legitimacy in England, however. Simon had called before the meeting to propose that the whole of the JKS GB & Ireland threaten to resign if the Headquarters followed through with their suspension of me.

'If you make that proposal,' Peter replied, 'then you and I have a problem'.

Powerless to alter the course of events, Simon attended the meeting without optimism.

Peter commenced proceedings. 'He simply shouldn't have written the book.' (He didn't tell them he had read the book six years ago and had had no complaints then.)

'So, business as usual, then,' another instructor chipped in, as if on cue. Peter nodded his approval. Simon looked around the room to see many heads dropped, unwilling to meet anyone's gaze.

'Do you have anything to say, Simon?'

'No!' came the reply. He stood up, left the meeting and walked away from the JKS for ever.

A week after my resignation email to Japan, the Headquarters responded to the world. I never received anything, but I was, secretly, forwarded the offending email by several JKS friends. I opened it and for the first time ever I read a Headquarter email without a nervous knot in my stomach. Their ownership of me had expired. I was free.

They wished to inform the JKS world that they were not prepared to accept my resignation from the group and instead expelled me. I laughed, but then read on. They wanted to let everyone know why I had been suspended and had attached a copy of my manuscript, encouraging instructors to read and judge for themselves. How dare they? The perfect combination of arrogance and ignorance. It was one thing to publicly try to execute my reputation, but to publish my copyrighted material was insane; surely even they saw the illegality of it. I contacted my lawyer immediately and an email was quickly sent demanding they delete all copyrighted material forthwith and instruct all international affiliated groups to do the same. Failure to do so would result in litigation. Within an hour Takahashi Sempai replied saying he had complied. Of course the damage had been done, but I wasn't going to take it any further. It did show to what lengths they were really prepared to go. In spite of all this I allowed myself a smile. Was this their game? I spoke to my friend in Denmark.

'You know, Scott,' he said with justifiable authority, 'they won't be happy until you are nothing, just teaching in a small hall to a handful of students'.

'You've known me since I was sixteen,' I replied. 'Do you think that will ever happen?'

'No.'

He was right. They would be like a dog with a bone and gnaw away at this problem indefinitely, but if this was their level of diplomacy, their level of PR, it would be an uphill struggle. I went back and studied the entire email from Yumoto Sensei to the JKS world. It mainly centred on their claims that I misrepresented my graduation of the Instructors' Course. They focused on my 'emotional email' and 'low standard' instead of explaining why they had promoted and endorsed me as a graduate of the course for five years after leaving Japan, and in some instances longer than that, including only nine months ago when they had allowed me to grade to 6th dan outside Japan. It was a joke and I knew the vast majority of instructors would see it as such. They only had to tell one lie for them to be liars. I just held my form and looked forward.

JKS GB & Ireland dojo heads started to contact me. 'Okay we're in' they would say and somewhere in my brain there would be a flicker of light amid the intense darkness and gloom. Within weeks about 60 per cent of the Irish membership had confirmed they would follow me. England was a little different. After Simon's immediate departure, about 20 per cent followed and by the end of February I counted thirty clubs in the newly formed WTKO GB & Ireland. It was early days, but it was a good start. Still, the waves of disappointment crashed over me with surprising regularity. I still regularly met Maz for lunch. She had quit karate long ago (something to do with having four kids) but she was still my closest of friends and a trusted confidante.

'What do you expect,' she said with wisdom and a smidgeon of impatience as I lamented my loss. 'You've just spent the last decade selling the JKS to the membership. They believed it hook, line and sinker. Now you are surprised some of them want to stay with this mythical organization you've created?'

She was right. I had championed the group as far and as wide as possible. I had protected my members from the bullshit and bickering that was a constant drain on my sanity. They were heavily invested in this reality and it would take far more than my current dilemma to jolt them from this truth. Despite this, I wanted to shake them, shock some sense into them. The group they believed in was a fiction: surely such a benevolent group wouldn't treat me in the way they had? But I couldn't challenge their choices, and it was their path, not mine. I realized that people I had called close friends were now forbidden from contacting me. They weren't even able to 'like' a Facebook post – apparently 'Japan was watching'! I accepted it and was thankful to the ones who did support me. This, of course, was how I felt at the best of times. At the worst of times, I was heartbroken, at sea, lost without hope of discovery. Harry took the news hard. Shortly after my resignation it came to a head during morning training. He was my friend, a strong, clever man who found it hard to conceal his disappointment.

'What could I have done, Harry? I tried everything.'

'You could've taken your punishment,' he said, and meant it.

Within a week he decided to take a break. Richard followed shortly after. Thomas was worried about them, but was far less invested in the JKS. A hastily arranged course with Richard Amos was scheduled in late February. Thomas as well as several other committed members had planned to grade in March with Yumoto Sensei. I had to do right by them, so managed to get Richard Sempai to my dojo for a midweek session and examination. One dojo head successfully graded to 5th dan, likewise another student passed 3rd dan. But Thomas messed up his grading and failed 4th dan. He, too, took a break.

At the beginning of April, not having seen them for six weeks, I got an email from Harry and a text from Richard – they had decided to stay with the JKS. I was understanding but concerned that, whilst training with me, they wouldn't be able to stay below the radar; the JKS were now keeping track of all their members. Thomas decided to come and tell me face to face. He stood in my office and informed me they had set up a JKS-affiliated dojo themselves. The three weren't particularly motivated to train with Fergus, so they were sweating it out, a trio of middle-aged men in a squash court somewhere in the suburbs.

'Thank you for coming to tell me.' It took every ounce of determination to suppress my anguish, 'But you have to understand that the news is devastating.'

'You'll be all right. I have to support Harry and Richard.'

'You think I'm all right?' I asked. Every time one of my friends turned their back on me it was another knife wound, another cut, which oozed black, depressing sludge.

He gave me a hug, said, 'I know you'll be okay,' and walked out. I only saw Thomas once again. Several months later he turned up one evening to hand back his and Harry's keys for the dojo. I congratulated him on their 4th dan promotion, which had been all over Facebook.

'It was surprisingly easy,' he said, as if it would have been anything else. The Headquarters had continued their character assassination of me, most of which, fortunately, would be dismissed by any rational person. In the Headquarters' version of the truth, no one had followed me and Takahashi Sempai's killer blow was, 'Look, even his own students are leaving him!' My three friends gave him that ammo and he used it well.

'But you know what,' Thomas continued, as if we were two old housewives gossiping over recent events, 'Fergus's organizational skill ...' He smirked.

'Thomas, I don't want to know. That group he is destroying represents over a decade of my life. It was taken from me and handed into the incapable mitts of Fergus. *I don't want to know*!' He left, never to be seen again.

By the beginning of March cancellations for courses were coming in thick and fast. I looked at my wall calendar and wiped out every seminar I had planned with JKS affiliates. I literally wiped out a year's salary, thousands of euro. Five remained out of the forty that had been booked. The first was an independent group in Wales. By chance, they had also booked Matt Price, so we made our way there separately. I stood in the dojo, waiting for my friend to arrive. He walked in, saw me and looked away. Then, fidgeting a little, he came over.

'Hi mate,' I said, as upbeat as possible.

'Yeah, all right ... I guess we better get started.'

Wow. Even Matt had been affected. The course commenced, the group was split and I did my thing, Matt did his. At the end the local instructor called us all in for a group photo. I stood at the end of the line as Matt moved out of shot. A photo was taken, then I was asked to move as Matt jumped in.

'Really? You aren't even allowed to have a photo with me?' He shrugged, wary of the obvious phone call he had received when Peter saw on Facebook we would be teaching together.

The following week Yumoto Sensei made his annual trip to the UK and Ireland. It was weird that he was in Dublin, so close, but with a Berlin Wall of animosity separating us. He then flew to the UK and held a meeting with JKS GB & Ireland dojo heads. William Sensei flew in from South Africa to add further gravitas to the occasion – the big guns were out. Yumoto Sensei read a prepared statement, which denounced me as a liar, traitor and a man without honour. What could I expect? Both sides were becoming entrenched. However, in

Looking relaxed with Simon (front row, far right) at Keio University, Tokyo, Japan, October 2015.

the audience were friends and dojo buddies. One attendee was one of my original instructors. A very senior 7th dan, I had known him since I was a kid. Whilst Yumoto Sensei talked about his former student, he sat by passively, not saying a word. I felt sick when I heard about him and many other strong men who sat back and allowed the Headquarters' version of the truth spill out in front of them, toxic waste that lapped at their feet. What was worse? What was said of me or people's acceptance of it? I was, and still am, unsure. But losing friends taught me a valuable lesson: moving forward I would never hide the whole truth from people, my group would get it warts and all. I would build a community that was loyal to each other and not loyal to a remote group that didn't deserve such dedication. We could only be strong together.

While this was going on I occasionally lurched from despair to sheer delight. Clubs in England and Ireland gave me their undying support. It was hugely rewarding to know that some friends saw my truth and stood by me. This was replicated in other countries, where my resignation seemed to act as a catalyst for affiliates in several European countries who finally saw an alternative to the increasingly dictatorial nature of Takahashi Sempai and the JKS. The WTKO had a solid foundation, developed since the turn of the millennium, on which we started to have an input.

At the same time the garbage being spouted by the JKS was so ridiculous that it played into our hands. Their outbursts reinforced what I was saying. At one point they emailed around to tell affiliates that they had decided to retract my 6th dan, something I had been awarded a year ago, but failed to refund me. It showed them to be petty and puerile. They then sent out a further email listing JKS members who had 'liked' my *Karate Stupid* Facebook page, insisting that affiliate heads tell their students to 'unlike' it. They even posted a review of my book on Amazon, giving it a one-star rating, saying it was full of lies. Despite their less than subtle attempts at subterfuge, my book was doing exceptionally well. It was getting five-star review after review and was number one in Amazon's Martial

Arts category for most of the year. It also got to number seven in the Sports Autobiographies section – I was sandwiched between Mike Tyson and Sir Alex Ferguson, somewhere I never thought I would be. As a result I started to get invites from independent clubs and groups. Sometime in late spring I was again standing in my living room ironing T-shirts, my form of meditation. The wounds caused by Thomas, Richard and Harry still oozed and negative emotions sneaked up on me like ninjas in the night. 'Enough,' I said to myself. I had the love and support of my family, the backing of a group of friends, sempai and sensei who were behind me 100 per cent, plus the group was growing and gaining momentum. Enough of the self-pity. Something clicked inside, a determination that had been honed by the very sempai who sought to destroy me. Onwards and upwards!

It is two years to the day from when I was first suspended. So much has happened. The WTKO GB & Ireland has gone from strength to strength. We now have sixty-three clubs and have created a community so strong that nothing will break it. Senior JKS members from England and Scotland subsequently left and joined us on our journey. Dojos in Wales also joined and with senior members of the Irish Karate community coming on board as well, we are now a major player within the British Isles. The WTKO worldwide continues to grow and the JKS is a distant memory, one that is occasionally forced to the forefront, but not by my doing. Last year, after deleting so many courses, I ended up doing thirty-five gigs. This year I have just finished my fiftieth. I never dreamed I could be so busy. It has come together in a way that is beyond my wildest dreams and has obliterated the nightmare that plagued me two years ago. Albeit born from insecurity, my ideas of finding a third way have been proven good. My blind spot before was underestimating the influence of Japan and others who didn't follow this ethos; lesson learnt.

In October I made a welcome return to Japan. It was strange to be wandering around Tokyo as my merry band of karate ducklings waddled behind me, like I was doing something illicit. We trained at Keio University, Funakoshi Sensei's first dojo, with instructors who began training with the Shotokan founder. I felt I had to prove myself every time. One instructor broke my nose as he countered my pre-arranged attack, but it was worth it. Some great and some fierce masters taught my group authentic karate and afterwards would often sidle up to me.

'Scott Sensei, you have a great sense for karate, you are welcome back anytime,' a former world champion said.

'Scott Sensei, you are the real deal,' a national *kata* champion added.

We kept our training schedule secret – I wasn't stupid. The day we left Tokyo I gave my group the nod and they posted marvellous reports and gushing praise for the trip on Facebook. The day after, Yumoto Sensei rang Keio University. 'Please don't have anything to do with Scott,' he asked. 'Please don't let him train at Keio.'

'I'm sorry,' they replied. 'We will continue our friendship.' Not everyone can be told what to do.

'May you live in interesting times' is a Chinese proverb – perhaps a curse, I'm not sure. And so, with that cosy little anecdote, let's finish here, shall we?

After all, the ultimate revenge is happiness.

POSTSCRIPT

1 April 2016

My nose is useless. After years of putting it in front of too many fists, the cartilage is mangled. In the autumn of last year Tor had had enough and ordered me to the doctor, unable to cope with my inability to sleep without snoring loud enough to wake the dead. Sleep clinics, MRI scans and jaw protrusion devices were ordered. However, the neurology department called me back. White spots on my brain had been 'accidentally' found. A further scan was ordered six months hence. I waited, trying not to Google 'lesions', 'early onset Alzheimer's' and 'multiple sclerosis'.

Last month I had my follow-up appointment with the professor of neurology.

'Don't worry,' he smiled. 'These spots are in the wrong place to be problematic.'

'So what caused them?' I asked.

'Have you ever been hit really hard on the head?'

The Instructors' Course – the course that keeps on giving.

Made in the USA
Middletown, DE
18 August 2023

36920523R10136